EDWARD BOND

Saved

with commentary and notes by
DAVID DAVIS

BLOOMSBURY
LONDON • NEW DELHI • NEW YORK • SYDNEY

Bloomsbury Methuen Drama

An imprint of Bloomsbury Publishing Plc

50 Bedford Square
London
WC1B 3DP
UK

1385 Broadway
New York
NY 10018
USA

www.bloomsbury.com

Bloomsbury is a registered trade mark of Bloomsbury Publishing Plc

Saved first published in the United Kingdom in 1966 by Methuen and Co. Ltd
This edition first published in the United Kingdom in 2009 by Bloomsbury Methuen Drama
Reprinted 2012 (twice), 2013

British Library Cataloguing-in-Publication Data
A catalogue record for this book is available from the British Library.

ISBN: PB: 978-1-4081-0010-3

Library of Congress Cataloging-in-Publication Data
A catalog record for this book is available from the Library of Congress.

Typeset by Country Setting, Kingsdown, Kent
Printed and bound in Great Britain

Contents

First of all, I am indebted to Edward Bond, who has read several drafts and with extreme care and patience, responded to all the queries I have sent him.

I want to thank Gavin Bolton who also read and commented on a draft.

My thanks also to Chris Cooper, Bill Roper and my wife, Elaine, who read partial drafts and as usual gave invaluable feedback.

D.D.

Edward Bond

I was born at 8.30 p.m. on Wednesday the 18th July 1934
In a thunderstorm
An hour before her labour began my mother scrubbed the stairs to
    her flat to clean them for the midwife to tread on
In the district in which my mother lived medical people were
    regarded as agents of authority
I was first bombed when I was five
The bombing went on till I was eleven
Later the army taught me ten ways to kill my enemy
And the community taught me a hundred ways to kill my neighbour
I saw there was not justice between one part of the community and
    another
An injustice is like a pebble dropped in the centre of the ocean
When the ripples reach the shores they have turned into tidal waves
    that drown cities
Necessity rules our days by the law of cause-and-effect
Those who govern do not know what a person is
And the governed do not know what a government should be
Instead the evil do evil and because there is no justice the good must
    also do evil
How else can they govern the prison they live in?
I walked the streets and raged
I wanted the stones in the military cemetery to weep for the dead
    beneath them
I wanted the skull to dream of justice
And then I remembered the iron kite that flies in the child's mind
And saw the old touch their white hairs as gently as a sparrow
    nesting on the side of an iceberg
So at twenty I wrote a play
The law of plays must be cause-and-use
To break necessity and show how there may be justice
Like all who lived at the midpoint of this century or were born later
I am a citizen of Auschwitz and a citizen of Hiroshima

Of the place where the evil did evil and the place where the good did
    evil
Till there is justice there are no other places on earth: there are only
    these two places
But I am also a citizen of the just world still to be made
(Bond, 2000, *The Hidden Plot*, p. 2)

You tell me people want to know more of me personally. What is to
tell is simple. The mystery is that there is no mystery. I am the most
uninteresting of people. My *situation* may be interesting. The
totality of that can be told briefly.

My family are working class. My birth certificate describes my
father as a labourer. My mother left school when she was
fourteen. She was sent away five miles down flat fen roads to be a
skivvy in a farmhouse. I took her back there fifty years later. She
did not even look at the house. Why should she? Every Sunday to
see her family she walked five miles two ways. A few years ago a
grizzly Tory cabinet minister attacked the unemployed for
complaining at being unemployed. He told them to be like his
father: 'Get on yer bike and look for work.' My family could not
afford bikes. In the Depression my parents moved to London in
time for the war. I had almost no formal education. I left school at
fifteen – I just caught the extra year added by the Attlee
government. When I was enlisted in the infantry I was set an
intelligence test. Looking at the pages of complicated maths and
scientific formulae I was disturbed to see the extent of my
ignorance. At that time no one of my class could have learned
about such things. There was a sheet of less recherché questions.
One asked what is the opposite of heaven. It helpfully said that the
opposite began with 'h'. Quite unselfconsciously I wrote 'Hades'.
Somehow, I had picked up some sort of knowledge. Recently one
of my plays was staged in Dublin. The theatre called me (it is not a
lie, only publicity) the most influential British playwright of all
time. The interesting thing is that it could even be said about
someone of my origins. (Letter to David Davis, 19 May 2008)

[Edward Bond left school with no qualifications. He helped his
father, who was a panel beater, to prepare the cars for painting after
they had been in crashes – sanding them down.] 'I used to help him
at weekends and bloody hard work it was too.' (Bond, interview
with David Davis, 2008)

1953–5 National Service.

And then I went into the army. And they were obviously very confused about me because I had no education and they showed me all these exam papers, tests and so on. There were literary ones and then ones which were obviously foreign languages ones and then ones that were to do with very complicated maths. I just stared at it. I had absolutely no idea. And then I turned over [and it asked] two and two what do they equal and I put four and put a little note at the bottom: 'in most cases' [...] I must have been a precocious little sod [...] most of them I couldn't answer.

I quite liked being in the army... we went abroad, we went ski-ing, saw all the snow up in the mountains, never killed anybody. I liked that but I hated the army set-up. [...] There was the sergeant-major could just [pick on] individuals and they would sort of load them up with backpacks, with iron, incredibly heavy. The sergeant-major would have a stick under his arm. He'd make the guy run in front of him then he'd scream 'Halt' and the guy'd have to march on the spot then he'd stroll up and give him another order. The poor guy was like a donkey covered with sweat. There seemed to be a class of regular soldiers who almost seemed to be there for the punishment. I found it absolutely objectionable that human beings should treat somebody else like that. [...] I wanted to write about those things. So when I got out I started to write. [...] I decided to write this novel and I began it with the words, 'The end', because I had read James Joyce. I used to go to the library and borrow books before I went into the army. My mother didn't like this because she said I'd catch something from them. It really actually disturbed her [...] she worried about me.

[...] And so I started to write plays. I think they were pretty awful, but they were very strange. [...] I'd write page after page after page and then I'd throw them all away. I think I filled whole notebooks with nonsense, I mean not even English, making up a language which didn't mean anything, just sort of noise. [...] I decided that I'd better write in English but no sentence would be more than five words long. So I wrote quite a lot of plays in which no sentence was more than five words long. And then I got very fanatical and I started writing plays in which no sentence was more than five syllables long. I found I could cheat because really I was taking one sentence and dividing it up and just putting full stops. And I said, no, this is wrong – you've got to be able to produce a

thought in five words. I think it was very good training so that when
I did get a play that I'd written, although the play was derivative
and not interesting, not good, it was very well written. I thought
that was interesting. [...] I sent it to the [Royal] Court because that
was going to be the place [which welcomed new playwrights] and
George Devine wrote and said would I come and meet him. I went
along to see him. [There were] tiny little pokey offices, nothing like
the place they've got now, and I was shown into a room and he was
sitting behind his desk and had his pipe and he said 'Sit down'. I sat
down and there was this long silence – he just looked at me.
Afterwards I learned that was him – he would want you to make the
first move. He just looked at me for what seemed like a century and
I didn't know what to do and I just waited. He must have thought,
'Come on you should have spoken by now,' but I just looked at
him. He took his pipe out of his mouth and tapped the script on the
desk in front of him, and it was my script. He tapped it and said,
'Did you write that?' I thought, 'Oh my god, he's going to call for
the police or something. He thinks it's obscene.' I gulped and said,
'Yeh.' And, again, there was this long silence. He expected me to
talk about it. Then he took his pipe out of his mouth again and he
said, 'It means absolutely nothing to me.' I remember his words
precisely, 'It means absolutely nothing to me.' He put his pipe back
in his mouth and stared at me again. I thought, sod you mate, and
so I said, 'If you don't take a puff of your pipe it'll go out.' He
obviously thought he had to regain authority and so he took his
pipe out of his mouth and sort of flicked it [the script] open with the
end of his pipe and I thought, fine, now you're going to put your
spit over it. And then he turned it round, using his pipe and said,
'Read that page.' I read it and half way through, I didn't know if I
was making much sense of it, [I thought] do I turn the page over at
the bottom or whatever? I thought, what is the middle-class
etiquette in this situation? I got to the end of the page and finished
in mid sentence. He looked at me and said, 'It seems to mean
something when you read it. You'd better come and work here,' and
I thought that was such an extraordinary remark; that he could be
so open to something that was new to him. It shows why he had
such a creative influence on British theatre. I said, 'I'm working in
this factory,' and he said, 'Do you want to be a writer or not?' And I
said, 'Yeh.' He said, 'Well take your holiday. [...] You can be a
member of the writers' group and you ought to come and see some
rehearsals.' I said, 'Fine.' He had this list in front of him and said,

'When can you get a holiday?' and I said, 'In about two weeks' time.' He looked at the plan and said, 'I might find something that would interest you. Orson Welles is directing here in a few weeks' time. Would you like to see that?' Being uppity I said, 'What's he directing?' He said, 'He's directing Laurence Olivier.' And I said, 'Yes, well I'll come along.' So the first rehearsal I ever saw was Orson Welles directing Laurence Olivier. Then I joined the writers' group. They all thought I was very odd because I ran everywhere. The reason I ran everywhere was because I was working and I had to run to get there on time. It was very useful. They made us do an improvisation. [...] And afterwards they all said, 'You can do it. You're good at that.' And I found that you could just put yourself in the situation and let the situation tell you what it needed and then the rest followed. [...] I wrote *Saved* and sent it to them and it was in a drawer for about two years. (Ibid.)

1958	Invited to join Royal Court writers' group. This lasted two years. He also read plays for the Royal Court.
1958–62	Part of Royal Court community of artists and during this period wrote fifteen plays for stage and TV.
1962	Club performance of the first play he has wanted to 'own', *The Pope's Wedding*.
1964	*Saved* written. Performed on 3 November 1965 – censor cut whole of Scenes Six and Nine and demanded many more cuts.

I now had a reputation for having written a very violent play – well, Hollywood is interested, isn't it. I didn't have an agent. I'd read somewhere that Bernard Shaw had never had an agent and so I thought, well fine, if he didn't need one then I don't need one. So I was writing this stuff and getting absolutely no money for it. It was ridiculous. I can't remember what it was but I wrote this script and they were very disappointed and said, 'But it's not violent.' It didn't have blood and gore all over the place, so that didn't go very far. Then I did get involved in a couple of other films. Again, I didn't have an agent. I wrote these scripts. I get no money for *Blow Up* and I get no money for *Walkabout*. I got money when I first did it but I don't have any residual rights. [Bond won an Oscar nomination for *Blow Up*.]

Then I wrote some other films: *Laughter in the Dark* and so on. They were none of them my films. I had no control over them. But my life changed. I was a professional writer. There were productions abroad and it was mainly from these that I earned a living as a writer. And also I did some directing. I bought this house so that I could live here and write. (Ibid.)

1967   Bond's third play *Early Morning* banned outright.
        Stage censorship ended.
1968   George Devine Award for *Saved*.
        John Whiting Award for Most Promising Newcomer.
1971   Marries Elisabeth Pablé.
1976   Obie Award for *Bingo*.
1977   Hon. D.Litt., Yale University.
1977–9 Northern Arts Literary Fellowship.

[Peter Hall invited Bond to go and direct his plays at the National Theatre and this relationship lasted until the 1980s when Bond found he could no longer work there. He found a totally different approach to drama there to the one he had had at the Royal Court and a totally different ethos. He ended this working relationship and not long after started working with La Colline theatre in Paris, part of the French National Theatre.]

My ambition is to write better. My ambition is to understand more than I can understand. My need is for time to be able to do that. [...] What I should like to do is create worlds that people can inhabit and situate their own life in those worlds. I don't mean copy what's in the world, I just mean open a space for them to use – to really use practically. Not to think this is odd, this is sacred ground. It's more than sacred. It's more important than sacred. It is human. That's the story of my life. (Ibid.)

1978   Directs the first modern play on the Olivier stage at the
        National Theatre – his own play *The Woman*.
1990s   Starts long-term working relationship with Big Brum
        Theatre in Education company, becoming their drama
        consultant.
2007   City of Lyon Medal for his contribution to French theatre.

I am the most anonymous, ordinary person. I have met no one who 'counts' (I don't mean mathematicians), don't mix in literary circles, find professional 'trade talk' tedious, avoid 'dinner parties' and 'cocktail parties'. I had assumed that if I ever became performed I would 'get invitations' and enter middle-class circles, but I found the people in them aggressive and frightened and so I avoided them. I have a few close friends (who tend to be absolute experts in subjects that I need, and I am in awe of their knowledge). I dislike fussy complicated food. I cannot get over the shock of burning St Joan but now you can sit and, shockingly, have coffee on the square where she was burnt. I am shocked by people who are destructive on principle, but I would like to be too worldly-wise to be shocked, astonished by anything I come across (but I know that's impossible) but be delighted by many things. I admire kindness, patience, application and sensitivity in others, and I seem unjustifiably happy and hope to write better. I am encouraged by the fact that I never understood anything till I was sixty-eight. (Letter to David Davis, 29 March 2008)

I was once [interviewed] by a German reporter. She came in. I always remember she was wearing a two-piece suit, brown-coloured. She sat down and flicked open her notebook. It was before the days of recorders I suppose. She produced a pencil and she said, 'Now Mr Bond, will you please tell us what we have to do to save the world, but can you make it quick as I've only got ten minutes.' If she'd given me fifteen minutes, history would have been changed but she only gave me ten minutes so I failed. (Bond, interview with David Davis, 2008)

List of first performances

9.12.1962	*The Pope's Wedding*
3.11.1965	*Saved*
13.1.1966	*A Chaste Maid in Cheapside* (adaptation)
18.4.1967	*The Three Sisters* (translation)
31.3.1968	*Early Morning*
24.6.1968	*Narrow Road to the Deep North*
22.3.1970	*Black Mass* (part of *Sharpeville Sequence*)
11.4.1971	*Passion*
29.9.1971	*Lear*
22.5.1973	*The Sea*
14.11.1973	*Bingo: Scenes of Money and Death*
28.5.1974	*Spring Awakening* (translation)

2007   *Tune*
2008   *People* (one of the Colline pentad)
        Innocence (one of the Colline pentad – written 2008)

Other publications

1978   *Theatre Poems and Songs*
1987   *Collected Poems 1978–85*
1990   *Notes on Post-Modernism*
1994–2004   *Letters* (5 vols.)
1995   *Notes on Imagination*
2000   *The Hidden Plot: Notes on Theatre and the State*
2000   *Selected Notebooks* vol. 1
2001   *Selected Notebooks* vol. 2

Plot

Scene One
The living room of Pam's house. Len comes back with Pam to her house. They settle down in an attempt to have sex on the sofa. Pam's dad comes in and goes straight out. Len is uncomfortable but Pam is not. Her dad is late going to work. Len wants to wait until he's left the house. He has one of Pam's cigarettes but forgets to offer her one. Pam is still lying there ready for sex. Len urges her to do her dress up in case someone comes in. Len wants to stay the night but Pam says no. They joke about sex. They pretend to be having sex by eating sweets loudly so that her dad can hear. Harry (her dad) puts his head round the door. He eventually goes to work and they get ready to have sex.

Scene Two
Park. Pam and Len are in a rowing boat. Len has moved in as a lodger. They talk of marriage, doing up a house and Pam knitting a sweater for Len. Pam reveals she had a brother, killed by a bomb in the war. Len asks about her parents never speaking to each other. Fred (in charge of the boats) calls them in and makes 'advances' to Pam. Len takes it with humour.

Scene Three
Park. Pete, Barry, Mike and Colin are passing time during their lunch break. Pete has witnessed a boy run over by a lorry. He claims he speeded up to drive at the boy and hit him so that the boy went under the lorry. Barry doesn't believe him. The others claim he wouldn't have the guts to do something like that. Barry claims he's shot 'yeller-niggers'. They bandy small talk of sex and make bad jokes. Len comes in. Colin recognises him. They were old school mates. He is waiting for Mary (Pam's mother). Len helps her with her shopping bag. They pretend to think it's his girl-friend and make sex jokes. Len shrugs it off with humour. They go back to work.

Scene Four

The living room. Harry is sitting in the dark nearly asleep. Mary comes in to lay the table and switches light on. She goes out. Harry turns it off. Mary comes in again to lay the table and switches light on again. She brings in Len's dinner. The TV is switched on. A baby starts to cry and cries all through the scene. Mary eventually calls on Pam to go to the baby. Pam turns up TV instead. It is not clear whose baby it is. Pam denies it's Len's. Pam is urging Len to move out and leave her in peace. Len won't leave the baby to be neglected. Fred comes round for Pam. He is late. Pam and Fred go out. Mary goes to bed. Harry tells Len he should close his door when Fred stays the night. Harry stays in his chair with the light out when the rest go to bed. The crying baby sobs itself to silence.

Scene Five

Len's bedroom. Pam is in bed – clearly not ill. Len gives her medicine and tucks the bedding in. Pam doesn't want him there. Mary calls up that Pam should be up and that food is on the table. Len goes out and comes back with the baby. Pam refuses to take it or look after it. Len tells her Fred is coming round. He has two tickets for Crystal Palace and has invited Fred so he'll have to come to the house. Pam will be able to see him. She says she'll have a wash to be ready for Fred.

Scene Six

The Park. Fred is fishing and Len watching. Len asks Fred if he is coming round to see Pam. He tells Fred he used to hear him in bed with Pam. They discuss their relationship with Pam. For Fred it is no more than a lay. Len makes no claims or demands. It comes out that Len only slept with Pam the one time. This makes it much more probable that Fred is the father. Fred teaches Len about fishing. Mike enters. He has also been fishing and caught nothing. He and Fred plan a night on the town. Pam enters with the baby in a pram and tries to persuade Fred to come round. Len points out she has left the brake off. The baby is silent as she has given it aspirins. Fred tells Pam he has finished with her. She storms off. Len follows to get her back. Pete and Colin enter followed by Barry. Eventually they start a 'harmless' game of pushing the pram to each other. The pushing of the pram becomes more violent. Fred and Mike are not involved. They are busy planning how to get sex that coming evening. Eventually the others pull the baby's nappy off. They spit at it and punch it. They wipe the contents of the nappy over the baby. Eventually Fred is goaded into throwing a stone at the baby. They all throw stones at it. They exit making 'buzzing' sound. Pam comes in and collects the baby without noticing anything.

Scene Seven
Fred is in prison. Women waiting outside have attacked him and spat on him. Pam is allowed five minutes to visit him. He blames her for his predicament. She shouldn't have had the baby, shouldn't have left it in the park and has ruined his life. She has not brought him any cigarettes either. Fred shows righteous indignation. Pam vows to stand by him. Len arrives with sixty cigarettes. Len reckons he'll get manslaughter. Len reveals he saw it all.

Scene Eight
The living room. Harry is ironing. Len tells him he ought to have left his wife. We learn Fred is coming out of prison soon. Pam comes in drying her hair. She picks on Len, accusing him of hiding her *Radio Times* and then anything else she can think of. It becomes clear she is preparing the way for Fred to move in when he comes out of jail.

Scene Nine
The living room. Len is cleaning his shoes. Mary is getting ready to go to the cinema. Len cleans Mary's shoes. There is banter with sexual overtones. She ladders her stocking on a chair. Len darns her stocking for her while it is still on. Harry comes in to do his pools. Len bites off the thread. Harry goes out. Len tries to persuade Mary to miss the cinema but she goes out. Len prepares to masturbate on the couch.

Scene Ten
A café. Pam and Len are waiting for Fred. He comes in with the other lads and Liz, his old girlfriend. They offer to stand him breakfast. It is clear Fred is playing the old lag. He tells prison jokes and anecdotes. Len wants to know what killing the baby was like. Pam keeps trying to persuade Fred to come back with her. Finally he storms out not waiting for the food. Len says he'll see Pam home and wants to know if they can start over again.

Scene Eleven
The living room. Harry is trying to get some bread and butter and tea. Mary keeps moving the teapot away from him claiming it is hers. The tension between them is played out by Mary moving things away from Harry. She pours his tea on the floor. A row breaks out over Len mending her stockings. Harry moves towards Mary but trips over a chair and breaks the chair leg off. Mary breaks the teapot over his head. Harry claims he is scalded. Len tries to help. Pam finds out from Harry what happened between Len and her mother. Pam is in hysterics and blames everything on Len. Len says he'll leave.

Scene Twelve
Len's bedroom. Len is lying on the floor with his head to the floorboards and a knife in his hand. Harry comes in looking like a ghost, with his head in bandages. Len is clearing the cracks in the floorboard with the knife to hear better. Harry tells him it is Pam crying, not someone in her room. Len is packing to leave. Harry tries to persuade Len not to leave. Harry and Len talk about Harry's life with Mary in earlier times. Harry reminisces about the war: 'Most I remember was the peace an' quiet.' He tells how he shot someone. He says he'll leave Mary once she's old and can't get anyone else. Len gets ready for bed. Offers aspirins to Harry for his head. Harry goes.

Scene Thirteen
The living room. The routine of the house returns on an even more deadly scale. The rows have stopped. Pam has her *Radio Times*. There is no communication now except for one attempt by Len. Len is mending the chair that broke in the earlier row.

Commentary

Bond, Brecht (and Stanislavski)

> If today *Saved* were offered to the Royal National Theatre as a new play
> it would refuse it as certainly as it refused *Coffee* and *Crime of the*
> *Twenty-first Century* [...] We are made not by our ability to reason but
> by our need to dramatize ourselves and our situations. In drama reason
> and imagination elucidate each other. This enables us to understand
> ourselves and what we do. Dramatization in all its forms is the one means
> we have of creating this knowledge and constantly recreating our
> humanness. (Bond, 2000: 1)

When I first read *Saved* many years ago, I remember nearly falling
off my chair laughing at some scenes and being very shocked by
others. It seemed a very straightforward play, easy to understand,
and one that should be quite easy to act. I had never seen a
performance until the recent excellent production at the Abbey
Theatre, Dublin, in 2008. It took a long time for me to understand
that beneath, or rather intrinsic to this play, was a whole new
approach to theatre: the beginnings of a whole new form of theatre.
I felt a bit ashamed of my simplistic, earlier response. I came face-to-
face with Edward Bond more than twenty years ago when he gave a
keynote address to a drama conference. I understood only half of
what he said and I realised that I needed to put in some serious
study time. The more I came to understand how his form of theatre
worked, the more the play unfolded before my eyes. My earlier
laughter sounded hollow in my ears: what did my laughter mean?
After some twenty years of first-hand contact with Edward Bond,
ten of those when he was patron of a drama centre I had helped to
set up,[1] I began to understand something of what he was pursuing.
He gave annual workshops or talks about his work to the students
at the Centre and I watched him at work with Big Brum Theatre in
Education company in Birmingham. I continually felt that I had
understood something and then something else would confuse and

[1] The International Centre for Studies in Drama in Education at the University of
Central England, now Birmingham City University.

intrigue me. I feel very much that I am still pursuing that understanding and it is in the spirit of someone keen to share their journey so far, that I approach this introduction; not as someone who has all the answers. What I want to do is share my understanding so far of how his theatre needs to be approached and some of the complexities of his theorising. My hope here is that this will stimulate the student reader to want to study more of Bond's plays and to tackle his theoretical writings. To provide a platform from which to do this is all that I can undertake to attempt.

Some of Bond's plays are comedies but others he specifically calls tragedies. He rejects the account of tragedy given by Aristotle and Brecht and says that without the Tragic there can be no moral order and so no humanness. The extreme tragic situation forces us to make a choice which either asserts our humanness or leads us deeper into corruption. Even if he had done nothing else, his restoration of the concept of the Tragic would have given him a major influence on modern drama. It makes it possible again for the stage to deal with the profoundest paradoxes of being human. He claims that the Tragic figures are always radically innocent and this is true of both Antigone and Medea: the woman who dies to honour her brother and the woman who murders her own children. This will be important to bear in mind as we study *Saved*.

In order to explore the play with the hindsight afforded to us by time, I intend to examine how Bond and Brecht approach the problem of ideology then, later, to set out key dimensions of the distinctly different approaches to theatre of Brecht and Stanislavski, and to contrast these with Bond's. It should be useful to find a way into Bond's theatre through this route of comparison and contrast. This will take us into the context in which *Saved* was first performed, which led to it being a *cause célèbre* and renewed the struggle against censorship. Finally, I offer a detailed commentary on the text itself.

I shall start with the last scene of *Saved*. A young man mends a chair in a living room as silent as a graveyard. It is a cultural graveyard. The silence is the silence of ideology. He says only one thing, he asks for help, and is ignored. Why has he chosen to live in a graveyard? He could live under better circumstances but he will have to make them. He is making a determined effort. But why does the play text give such intricate stage directions to Len in the final scene of *Saved*? There are two loud bangs off stage, then detailed directions as to how Len should engage with the broken chair.

He crouches. His head is below the level of the seat. [...] He rests his left wrist high on the chair back and his right elbow on the chair seat. His right hand hangs in space. [...] His head is sunk into his shoulders. [...] In one connected movement LEN *turns the chair upright and stands to his full height. He has grasped the seat at diagonally opposite corners, so that the diagonal is parallel with the front of his body. [...] He bends over the chair so that his stomach or chest rests on the seat.* (pp. 122–3)

These are only extracts from his stage directions. Why are they so detailed? He's only mending a chair. To find the answer to this question involves exploring the whole of Bond's dramaturgy. In these 'simple' stage directions can be found the key to the whole of Bond's theatre form.

One of the intriguing dimensions of writing about *Saved* in 2008 is that in the 1960s when the play was written, Bond had no worked-out theory of theatre nor had he begun the voluminous commentaries on his plays, on drama and society and the role drama has to play in our struggle for humanness.[1] Now, with hindsight, it is possible to see that all the key dimensions of his work have always been there, from the earliest published plays. I want to argue that it is impossible to understand the revolutionary nature of *Saved* (and his other plays) as a new form of drama, without taking some account of Bond's struggle to develop this new form of theatre, or as he would prefer to call it, drama. It is important to emphasise that he has developed a completely new form of theatre. This has been, and still is, his life's work.

Perhaps this is to put things back-to-front. Rather, Bond's life concern is with how humanness can be created, starting with his own humanness. This has, of necessity, taken him through a series of explorations in his plays to discover who he, himself, is and what is involved in working for his own worth as a human being. This has prescribed areas of exploration his plays have needed to enter, and in seeking to make his plays work in the same way for others, this has entailed developing theatre form.

Again, it is impossible to discuss Bond without relating him, contrasting him, to Brecht and Stanislavski. Many people see Brecht and Bond as comrades-in-arms with similar agendas. In many ways this is true. They would both have been in the same prison camp together under a fascist regime. Nevertheless, in theatre terms, the

[1] 'Interviewer: You can't have been able to articulate consciously, at that stage, what you were doing [at the time of writing *Saved*]. Bond: No.' (Bond, 2008a)

only area where this is true is that they are both fundamentally concerned with how to get round behind ideology in order to engage with objective reality. However, their methods are fundamentally different, opposites even. Would it be true to say that Brecht influenced Bond? After an initial, short-lived admiration of, for example, *Mother Courage*, Brecht's main use for Bond was as a stimulus to engage with form and to realise his own plays needed to work in a completely different way. Importantly, their approaches to what constitutes humanness is fundamentally different.

The problem of ideology

Below are a few of the many quotations it is possible to find, in fiction as well as in non-fiction, dealing with the problem of ideology. It is interesting that the area is so well known and yet we struggle even to recognise it.

> Ideology provides a lens through which one sees the world, a set of beliefs that are held so firmly that one hardly needs empirical confirmation. Evidence that contradicts those beliefs is summarily dismissed. (Stiglitz, 2002: 222)

> Between the experience of living a normal life at this moment on the planet and the public narratives being offered to give a sense to that life, the empty space, the gap, is enormous. (John Berger, quoted by Ali Smith in *The Accidental*, 2006, Harmondsworth: Penguin Books)

> Inside the sealed country, Stalin poured on the *old* death. In the West, the ordeal is of a *new* death. There aren't any words for what happens to the soul in the free world. Never mind 'rising entitlements,' never mind the luxury 'life style.' Our buried judgment knows better. All this is seen by remote centers of consciousness, which struggle against full wakefulness. Full wakefulness would make us face up to the *new* death, the peculiar ordeal of *our* side of the world. The opening of a true consciousness to what is *actually* occurring would be purgatory. (Bellow, 2007/1987: 93)

> We have no words to describe the reality of our lives. Which means we have no adequate language. (Bond, 2007)

> Democracy becomes the perfect form of slavery – imagination owned by the state. (Bond, 2000: 50)

The common problem (although problem doesn't capture the enormity of the task), that Bond and Brecht share, is to try to counter the mind control exercised by ideology over whole populations of people. Ideology is made up of a body of ideas and beliefs that a nation, a political system, a religion has about itself. The perpetuation and spread of these ideas and beliefs is fundamental to the continued existence of those who wish to spread their influence, either in pursuit of material or spiritual gain (most usually a combination of both) for their continued dominance. Ideology comes in the form of political doctrines such as communism or fascism, neo-conservatism or liberalism, patriotism or any form of religious belief system. This is what Bond calls the transcendental: any transcending system of ideas that draws large numbers of people into its domain. Usually a dominant ideology in a country is made up of a mixture of related ideologies: political, religious, and so on. Brecht, coming to maturity in the 1920s and 30s, was one of a whole mass of artists who were shattered by the way humans minds seemed to have been taken over to set human against human in the First World War.

Chomsky (2004) traces the growth of the need for governments to be mindful of the necessity to control public opinion. As part of the historical survey with which he opens his book, *Hegemony or Survival*, he quotes Walter Lippmann's essays on democracy written in the 1920s. Lippmann had been a member of Woodrow Wilson's[1] Committee on Public Information. He was regarded as a progressive thinker and won Pulitzer prizes for his writing. What was needed, he argued, was the manufacture of consent.

> This 'revolution' in the 'practice of democracy' should enable a 'specialized class' to manage the 'common interests' that 'very largely elude public opinion entirely'. [...] The 'responsible men' who are the proper decision-makers, Lippmann continued, must 'live free of the trampling and roar of a bewildered herd.' These 'ignorant and meddlesome outsiders' are to be 'spectators,' not 'participants.'
> (Chomsky, 2004: 6)

This was how a member of the Democratic Party, not a Republican, saw the 'person in the street', that is to say, us, 'the trampling and roar of a bewildered herd'. Today it is common knowledge that the first aim of most politicians is to work out how to 'spin' a particular

---

[1] Wilson was President of the USA from 1913 to 1921. He steered America into the First World War and was then awarded the Nobel Peace Prize in 1919 for setting up the League of Nations, the forerunner of the United Nations.

story so that reality is obfuscated and a false perspective put forward to shine an advantageous light on the particular area in question. The aim is to own people's consciousness.

This theme, the capture of minds, is explored by Dostoevsky in part of *The Brothers Karamazov*. Ivan tells his brother Alyosha the story of a long poem he has written. Jesus comes down to earth at the height of the Inquisition in the sixteenth century. (For some 600 years the Inquisition was the organ responsible for maintaining the Catholic faith and dealing with heretics.) The people immediately recognise Jesus and flock to him and he performs some miracles and through these acts they know he is the true saviour. The Grand Inquisitor observes him raise a girl from the dead and he recognises that he is indeed the true Jesus. Immediately, the Grand Inquisitor has Jesus arrested and thrown into jail. He comes to visit Jesus in prison and explains why he had him arrested. The Inquisitor tells him that during his forty days and nights in the desert, when he was tempted to prove who he really was by turning stone into bread and throwing himself from the spire of the temple so that angels would catch him, he made the wrong decisions. He should have performed miracles and then people would have followed him. Instead, he left them with the freedom of choice and this is what the Church has been battling with ever since. He could have saved people from themselves: people need authority and hate freedom. The Grand Inquisitor tells Jesus:

> There is nothing more seductive for man than the freedom of his conscience, but there is nothing more tormenting either [...] it was impossible to leave them in greater confusion and torment than you did, abandoning them to so many cares and insoluble problems. [...] There are three powers, only three power on earth, capable of conquering and holding captive forever the conscience of these feeble rebels, for their own happiness – these powers are miracle, mystery, and authority.
> (Dostoevsky, 2004: 254–5)

So the Grand Inquisitor has him burnt at the stake for threatening to undo all the good work they have been doing in wiping out freedom of choice and doubt.

Bond, reflecting on the power of ideology to control minds, states that 'Whoever owns nothingness owns you'. (After 'nothingness' is implied, 'and can envelop you in it'.) Humans are a meaning-seeking species. From our earliest origins we have looked up into the skies at the moon and the sun and wondered what is up there among the stars; sheltered from violent storms and thunder and lightning, fled from volcanoes, earthquakes and tornadoes and wondered what it all meant and made up myths to explain them to ourselves. We can do this because from our origins as a species we have had imagination. Later, many religions developed with creation myths and codes of human conduct. This all filled the void and prevented us from realising we are infinitesimal specks in a vast universe with no given meaning without the meanings we create. This is the area of Nothingness. It is the area where humans can explore their own destiny and those who claim to have the answers to the meaning of life can own nothingness and will own you if they can tie you in to it. The voice of the Grand Inquisitor, quoted above, claims, in the name of Christianity, that humans need to be given comfort and guidance, that they are afraid and lost if guidance and answers are not provided. Life is a mystery and death frightening. Humans need answers to what is out there beyond what Bond calls the Boundary of human knowledge. Bond's approach is the opposite of the Grand Inquisitor's. His plays seek to put us into the known-unknown so that we have to search out our humanity: that humanity which will force us to forge meanings and values that will give us a human, social future where we live in harmony with each other and in harmony with nature. Bond intends his drama not just to inform the audience, perhaps of something they did not know, but to oblige them to make a choice – to make choosing unavoidable. This was the struggle and purpose that Greek theatre found for itself and it is this journey which Bond continues and extends into our own age.

Brecht also took as his central target the struggle against what Marx called 'false consciousness'. 'Our society will not admit of its own accord what makes it move. It can even be said to exist purely through the secrecy with which it surrounds itself' (Brecht, 1978: 164). But this belief in a 'false consciousness' implies that Brecht, following Marx, believed a 'true consciousness' to be possible as an act of reason. Brecht's whole approach to his theatre was to lift that veil of secrecy so that humanity could see itself clearly. Reason and a critical eye were key to his approach. Bond's approach, however, is much more penetrating and radical. Far from there being a true consciousness that it is possible to find once we lift the scales from our eyes by an act of reasoning, Bond's view is that it is even possible to find ourselves in a worse place simply through reasoning alone. Reason may be captured by ideology. Hitler's Nazi Party was able to saturate the environment with an ideological view of Jews being to blame for the economic woes of German society in order to ensnare the desperate German people with a mixture of reasoning and emotion. The outcome of this sort of reasoning was Auschwitz, as Bond repeatedly points out. Reason without the struggle for human values, without human imagination to seek reason, can produce nuclear weapons, war and annihilation. This takes us into the crucial areas of difference between Bondian drama and Brechtian theatre. (Bond calls his 'theatre' drama to distinguish it from conventional theatre, but more of this later.) To explore this area it is necessary to take a short excursion into philosophy and linguistic theory.

Why a spade isn't a spade[1]

When we talk about someone who calls a spade a spade we tend to mean someone who is down-to-earth, a realist, who describes how things really are, who tells it like it is: they don't hide behind polite phrases to skirt around the truth of things. However, the relation between language and the world it purports to describe is far more complicated than this. Saussure pointed out that language is a system of arbitrary signs, a system of sounds, that bear no direct relation to what they are dealing with. The word apple is what we are used to in English but it is just an arrangement of some of the sounds available to the human larynx and by common agreement has come to stand for a particular fruit. I don't know what the Chinese word for apple is but I guess it will be nothing like the English word. In those countries far enough apart, totally different uses were made of the sounds humans could make and these developed into different languages. Where countries were closer or influenced each other, languages could be related into families of languages. However, the word apple in any language still only refers to the concept of apple we happen to have in our minds. That is, it does not refer to an object directly in the real world. The word apple is, in Saussure's terminology, a *signifier* and the concept in our head is the *signified*, but the actual apple we mean is the *referent* and there is no actual word for every apple in existence. In fact, we have no language for the particular, hence the struggle of artists to

[1] Acknowledgements to Magritte, who in 1936 painted a realistic painting of a pipe with the provocative title *Ceci n'est pas une pipe* (*This is not a pipe*). He was raising the same question about the relation of images and words to reality that I am raising here.

find ways to pierce the veil of generalities and give us the impression we know what they mean. The great gift of language is the ability to generalise that it gives us: its downside is that we are left thinking we know what someone is talking about, when in fact we are left with an abstraction, unless they give us the apple they are referring to. This, of course, is not possible once we start talking about society or justice or love. Thus, for example, justice is any personal/subjective meaning we have as the concept of justice: the bully gets his just deserts by receiving a caning, although this is another form of bullying. Here we are not touching objective reality at all but dealing with ideas. A spade is not a spade. Justice is really injustice. Himmler loved the German people which is why he killed the Jews. Love is not love. The way language only works with abstractions therefore allows people to use language to tell us how it is: to tell us what is real. If we allow ourselves to be taken into that way of thinking, then we are taken over by ideology. In fact, poststructuralists would argue that that is what happens once the newborn child leaves the early pre-linguistic stage and enters into the world given to him or her through language. Then the child takes in that culture and shapes itself and is shaped by it, as are we all. Bond has taken this dimension of poststructuralism into his thinking and structured his drama accordingly. His whole drama is structured to avoid this purely linguistic trap and enable the audience to 'see' with pre-linguistic/pre-encultured eyes, to avoid seeing through the opaque glasses of ideology. Strictly speaking this should be impossible but to find a form of doing so is Bond's pursuit. Brecht remained with the notion of a rational, thinking subject able to decide that a spade is a spade. Brecht is following Descartes, who in his Cogito claimed that inside us is a rational, thinking being. It will be important to open up these bald statements and justify them in what follows.

A brief dip into philosophy
Descartes (1596–1650) divided the person into a mind and a body: a dualist approach. His *Cogito ergo sum* (*Je pense donc je suis*: I am thinking therefore I exist) placed rational thought at the centre of existence. This was a revolution in the development of philosophy that was in tune with the Renaissance: the time of the conscious individual had arrived. The age of medieval intellectual slumber and strict stratification was over. It provided a bedrock belief that the

individual was the origin of ideas and fitted the growth of empirical natural science and gave reason the centre ground. The Age of Reason developed into the Enlightenment and on into modernity and Modernism. This still is probably the dominant way in which most people view themselves. The individual is the origin of ideas. Truth is seen as a subjective matter. Truth is the property of the individual. It is important to think for ourselves. Reason rules OK. This modernist philosophical base is Brecht's. However, poststructuralist thinking has undermined this certainty.

> Poststructuralism names a theory, or group of theories, concerning the relationship between human beings, the world, and the practice of making and reproducing meaning. On the one hand, poststructuralists affirm, consciousness is not the origin of the language we speak and images we recognize, so much as the product of the meanings we learn and reproduce. (Belsay, 2002: 5)

While poststructuralism is not one body of theory but, as Belsay points out above, a group of theories, what they have in common is the decentring of Descartes' Cogito, and the individual as the originator of his or her own consciousness. Building on Saussure's work on language,

> Truth and knowledge exist at the level of the signifier. In other words, truth is a matter of what we can say (or write, or indicate in diagrams or chemical symbols). If we lay claim to the truth, whether we conceive of this as objective or subjective, we are drawing on the big Other to do so. We are defining what we believe, that is to say, in terms drawn from out there, however much we seem to feel it in here. (Belsay, 2002: 73)

The big Other is Lacan's[1] term for all those social influences that shape and then saturate the very young child as s/he enters the world of language. Bond's work has been a life-long search for a drama form that enables us in the drama event to escape the social mind control of ideology constituted by language as described above and find drama experiences, drama events, moments of human interaction, which force us to 'think with our eyes' (to use a Bond phrase). While Bond accepts the advances that poststructuralist thinking has given us to see more clearly how culture and ideology can own us, he works against this control by moving us outside the

---

[1] Lacan (1901–81) was a highly influential French psychoanalyst who developed Freud's work.

domination of language by focusing the audience's attention on to objects and situations which can create Theatre/Drama Events and on to the 'invisible object'. However, again, more of this later.

All too generally it has not been recognised that what Bond has developed is new and requires a new understanding and that his theatre is fundamentally different to Brecht's. An example of this misunderstanding can be found in Eddershaw's (1996) book on Brecht. She finishes her book by looking at performing Brecht in the twenty-first century. She sees Bond's work as an extension of Brecht's.

> Recognition of Bond's contribution to the further development of a Brechtian form of theatre lies behind the continuing popularity of his plays on stage in Germany. (Eddershaw, 1996: 164)

Whether or not Bond has been misread in this way in Germany, I cannot say, but I can say categorically that Bond's work is not just a development of a Brechtian form of theatre. And again she comments:

> The ideas he [Bond] expresses in the notes constantly echo Brecht [These were notes Bond supplied to the Berliner Ensemble when they produced Bond's *Olly's Prison*.] [...] Bond [...] in his own plays employs what he calls 'aggro-effects' (a term that clearly echoes Brecht's *V-Effekt*). [Aggro-effect was an early term Bond used for what he has developed into a Theatre Event which he now calls a Drama Event.] (pp. 164–5)

Eddershaw's misconceptions about Bond's work can be seen echoed in students' work from other universities. For example, we find in a thesis posted on the internet:

> Bond's 'Agro Effects' are distinctly similar to Brecht's 'alienation effect' because they are a way of distancing the spectator from the action so they can rationalise about the events shown. [...] Nevertheless like Brecht, Bond understood that theatre and society constantly change and therefore he adapts Brecht's methods to fit in with his contemporary audience. (Mogose, 2007)

Neither of the above statements is true. The failure to recognise that his work is distinctly different to Brecht's has led to many of Bond's problems with the mainstream theatre, where directors and actors have repeatedly failed to do their homework and set about destroying his plays without realising it. This has been less true in France, especially at the Théâtre de la Colline, part of the French

National Theatre, where most of Bond's recent work for the large-scale theatre has been premiered.

Brecht and theatre

German theatre was vibrant in the period after the First World War. However, Brecht and like-minded young playwrights of his generation were totally dissatisfied with this theatre, one based on 'the spectator's ability to be carried along, identify himself, feel empathy and understand' (Brecht, 1978: 25). These new young playwrights wanted a theatre which could deal with 'the great themes of our times; as, for example, the building up of a mammoth industry, the conflict of classes, war, the fight against disease, and so on' (ibid., p. 77). Over a period of time Brecht began to develop his concept of the 'epic theatre', a term he first used in 1927 (ibid., p. 22). Writing in the same year Brecht points to its central feature.

> The essential point of the epic theatre is perhaps that it appeals less to the feelings than to the spectator's reason. Instead of sharing an experience the spectator must come to grips with things. At the same time it would be quite wrong to try and deny emotion to this kind of theatre. It would be much the same thing as trying to deny emotion to modern science. (Ibid., p. 23)

Willett (1967: 169) states that 'the basic meaning of "epic" [...] in Brecht [... is] a sequence of incidents or events, narrated without artificial restrictions as to time, place or relevance to a formal "plot"'. Emotions were part of this theatre as long as the playwright and the actors could control what they were. 'I laugh when they weep, I weep when they laugh' (Brecht, 1978: 71). The key thing is that empathy is ruled out. 'I'm for epic theatre! [...] to be presented quite coldly, classically and objectively. For they [the figures presented] are not matter for empathy' (ibid., p. 15).

This is a crucial aspect of Brecht's theatre and again, Bond's approach is different. In fact, Brecht's later plays tend to work against his own theory. How is it possible to witness Mother Courage having to refuse to recognise her dead son when the enemy troops bring him in and feel no empathy with her? Helene Weigel's silent scream at this moment must arouse empathy with her, as does the moment when Kattrin sacrifices her life to warn her mother and the town that the enemy are approaching. To write the play in this way (extremely sentimental though it is) and then deny the audience the human response of feeling with people in the impossible situations that society puts them in, is to attempt to dehumanise us. It is, as Katafiasz, points out, a classic double bind (Katafiasz, 2005: 30–1).[1] In a sense, Brecht is unable to stick to his own recipes. However, once again, Bond would not write these scenes in the same way, as they leave us with the empathetic/emotional state but without creating a problem for us, where we have to find out who we are in that moment.

So the search was on by Brecht to develop a form of epic theatre based on reason and criticism, made up of 'a mix of song; non-atmospheric lighting and a new type of curtain; projections of titles; elements of knockabout and music hall and deliberate measures by the actor to prevent himself and the audience from becoming caught up in the part' (Willett, 1998: 235). He began to read Marx in 1926 and had private lessons in Marxism. In Marx he found 'order and reason' (Fuegi, 1987: 48), interestingly, not humanity. Later, he found in behaviourist learning theory the same linear thinking which he pursued.

> We have acquired an entirely new psychology: viz., the American Dr Watson's Behaviourism. While other psychologists were proposing introspective investigation of the psyche in depth, twisting and bending human nature, this philosophy based itself solely on the human psyche's outward effects: on people's behaviour. [...] Once I've found out what modes of behaviour are most useful to the human race I show them to people and underline them. I show them in parables: if you act this way the following will happen, but if you act like that then the opposite will take place. (Brecht, 1978: 67)

Behaviourism is now an entirely discredited psychology. It is the way animals learn. Humans have a big C to put between stimulus and response: consciousness. That big C is the central difference between Brecht and Bond (and for Bond it is self-consciousness that is the key dimension). In the above quotation, Brecht reveals that he is interested in manipulating people as behaviourists would. No wonder he remained a Stalinist all his life.

His theatre then had to make his audience into spectators (again

---

[1] Like the mother who smacks the child and then tells her that she only did it because she loves her and it is for her own good. The explanation is counter-intuitive and confusing.

a word Bond would never use to describe his own audience), who were distanced from the action and whose reason would be engaged in relation to the events on the stage. Up until 1936, Brecht used the word *Entfremdung* for this, which is the word Marx and Hegel used to describe the alienation of humans from immediate connection and control over their lives caused by the social order in which they are forced to live. In 1935 Brecht met the Russian aesthetician Schklovski and was influenced by his term *priem ostrannenija*, rendering strange, making unusual (Fuegi, 1987: 82). Brecht adopted the term *Verfremdung*, which is a much more accurate word for what he was after, making the familiar strange and the strange familiar. However, 'alienation effect' has remained the translation for *Verfremdungseffekt*.

An important ingredient in this distancing was the epic style of acting. Central to this was finding the appropriate *gestus*. Brecht's use of the *gestus* defines the social attitude and focuses the attention on the class relationships and class forces. For example, a waiter, standing by a table, with notepad and pen, his whole being showing polite deference to the customer, no matter how difficult the customer is being, demonstrates a social *gest*. He is the servant of the customer, not an equal. If the customer, after her meal, turns in her seat, with her hands folded on her lap, ready to stand, she may be indicating to her partner that she is ready to leave and he is taking his time but it is not a social *gest*, it is a personal one. In Brecht's *Fear and Misery in the Third Reich* each scene is described as a social *gest*. The scene in a working-class home demonstrates resistance. The scene in the middle-class teacher's home demonstrates panic, fear and disintegration under the threat of danger.

The character is also written to discourage the audience forming any easy conclusion about him or her. In *The Caucasian Chalk Circle* Grusha is shown hesitating all night about whether or not to take the Governor's abandoned child with her. When at the end of the scene she scoops up the child and hurries off, this could be an altruistic act of human kindness. However, Brecht makes sure we know through the singer's commentary, that Grusha is in fact a thief and wants the baby for herself. This is the 'not-but'. The schoolteacher in *Fear and Misery* is not the in-control person he appears to be at first but a weak, vulnerable man. The working-class mother in the same play is not the mum easily manipulated by her daughter but a potential resistance fighter. Both exemplify a class relationship to the Third Reich, which is the *gestus*.

The overall presentation of his plays made use of *montage*, the juxtaposition of opposing or confirming points of view in the form of narration, a song, a title, a back projection, several of these possibly being employed at one and the same time. The epic style of acting involving centrally the *gestus*, along with the not-but and montage, are the fundamentals of Brecht's method.

I want to finish with a further commentary on Brecht's Marxism. It could be argued that he was never really a Marxist at all. He certainly took on a formal adherence to Marx's writings but I would want to underline the formal way in which he did this. It became dogma and was used as a series of mantras. The human dimension of Marxism was missing as I have tried to indicate above, with his excitement about behaviourism. I used the term 'linear thinking' above and by this I mean thinking that uses cold reason alone and leaves out the human dimension. This is how he could turn his back on empathy. He read Trotsky and yet ignored him. He remained a loyal Stalinist to the end. When the workers rose up against the reactionary 'communist' regime in East Germany, Brecht, who had been given a home for the Berliner Ensemble, wrote to Ulbricht, the East German communist leader, 'I feel it necessary at this moment to write to you and express my association with the SED [the East German Communist Party]. Yours, Bertolt Brecht' (Willett, 1964: 200). When Stalin died in 1953 he wrote, 'The oppressed of five continents [...] must have felt their hearts stop beating when they heard Stalin was dead' (ibid., p. 200). Brecht was very upset by Khrushchev's revelations about Stalin and turned to support Mao Tse-Tung (Fuegi, 1987: 171). Again, later, I want to contrast this with Bond's Marxism, which is qualitatively different.

After Brecht's death some notes were found which were published as *Appendices to the Short Organum*. In these notes he indicates that his approach to his theatre is changing. He no longer wants to call it 'epic theatre' but 'dialectical theatre' and his approach to the exclusion of empathy shows signs of weakening.

(a) However dogmatic it may seem to insist that self-identification with the character should be avoided in the performance, our generation can listen to this warning with advantage. However determinedly they obey it they can hardly carry it out to the letter, so the most likely result is that truly rending contradiction between experience

and portrayal, empathy and demonstration, justification and
criticism, which is what is aimed at.

(b) The contradiction between acting (demonstration) and experience
(empathy) often leads the uninstructed to suppose that only one or the
other can be manifest in the work of the actor. [...] In reality it is a
matter of two mutually hostile processes which fuse in the actor's work;
his performance is not just composed of a bit of the one and a bit of the
other. His particular effectiveness comes from the tussle and tension of
the two opposites, and also from their depth. (Brecht, 1978: 277–8)

If Brecht had not died at an early age, he might well have gone on to
develop his form of theatre in a different direction, although really
his creativity was curbed once he had his own theatre in East Berlin,
with a staff of some 200 people. Interestingly, the Communist Party
did not trust him enough to appoint him as head of his theatre: that
honour went to Helene Weigel, who remained a fiercely loyal
Stalinist and Party member all her life, an example of someone
taken over by ideology: the very sort of problem that Brecht set out
to deal with in his life's work. Somehow, he seems to have missed it
under his very nose.

In essence, Brecht deals with the objective, concentrates on the
social and leaves out the subjective. As we shall see, Stanislavski
deals with the subjective, concentrates on the personal and leaves
out the objective.

Stanislavski and theatre

It needs to be remembered that Stanislavski was first and foremost
an actor. He was not a playwright like Brecht and Bond, although
these two were also directors of their own work but as a secondary
activity. Stanislavski was involved from the word go with the actor's
art of bringing plays to life. The theatre that surrounded him as he
grew up was a theatre where the actors vied for centre stage from
which to declaim their lines in ringing tones, often after a prompt
from the side; a theatre where the actors left the stage without
turning away from the audience. Once Stanislavski had seen the
great Russian actor Shchepkin get inside the skin of a character, he
realised that his life mission was to bring realism to the Russian
stage: realism, not naturalism. Naturalism, for Stanislavski, was the
surface of life; realism was penetrating the 'historical and social
essence of events and characters' (Benedetti, 1982: 12).

He developed two distinct methods of acting: initially one
starting from the actor's emotional memory and then in the last five
years of his life the other, starting from physical actions: both these
methods within one system. Benedetti (1982) points to the six main
principles that were coming to underlie the system: getting to know
the play; the actor searching within himself for the psychological
material for the part; creating the inner and outer image of the
character by 'experiencing' it; physicalising the character;
synthesising the experiencing and the physicalising and then
working on the effect on the audience. It is one system because it
was the method of approach to gain this total effect that developed,
not a new system. The key point is that only one sixth of the work
was on the meaning of the play. Later, during a year's rehearsal,
when the Moscow Art Theatre had this amount of time to rehearse
a play, the first two months might be spent on discussing the play's
meaning but then the next ten months on working out how this
affected the through line development of the characters: the focus
was always on the acting.[1] In other words, the focus was always on
the psychology of the character.

In the first method, basing the actor's work on emotional memory:

> First the play was broken down, as usual, into segments. Each segment
> was then described in terms of the characters' psychology and the
> particular state they were in at any given moment. In each segment
> therefore the actor had a specific psychological goal to attain. For every
> action that was planned there was an inner-justification, springing from
> the total life of the character. [...] The sequence of psychological states
> reveals the total character which is, in turn, determined by the overall
> conception of the play. (Benedetti, 1982: 41)

This method of approaching a play, as Benedetti goes on to explain,
became one of finding the units, objectives and subtext, the through
line action and the superobjective.

Stanislavski was not interested in 'political' theatre if that meant
too much emphasis on the political content. An example of this can
be found in Stanislavski's disagreements with Nemirovich (co-
founder of the Moscow Art Theatre) when Nemirovich was
directing *Julius Caesar* and Stanislavski was playing Brutus.

---

[1] See Toporkov's (1998) book for a fascinating account of this. Toporkov joined
the Moscow Art Theatre for the last ten years of Stanislavski's life and chronicles
in very useful detail the rehearsal process. This was during the period when the
method of physical acting was being developed.

Stanislavski had wanted more psychological depth, more scope to explore the inner life of Brutus. Everything had been sacrificed to Nemirovich's concept of the play as political drama. (Benedetti, 1991: 151)

This example gives us a clue as to the reason why Stalin looked indulgently on the Moscow Art Theatre,[1] which was adopted as the official theatre of the Soviet Union. It posed no threat. Stalin even had the Red commissar removed from the theatre so that it could become autonomous and directly responsible to the Soviet Government. Clearly, this lack of focus on how the social enters into our lives contrasts with the approaches of both Brecht and Bond.

In the last few years of his life Stanislavski revised his approach and developed his second method: the method of physical action.[2] Toporkov tells of rehearsing the part of Chichikov in Gogol's *Dead Souls* and at one point in the rehearsal Toporkov says, 'I think that here Chichikov feels…' and Stanislavski replied, 'Don't think of that, think of how he *acts*' (Toporkov, 1979: 85). Benedetti points out the same thing during a Stanislavski rehearsal of *Tartuffe*, his final production.

Once someone asked 'What is the nature of the "emotional states" of the actors in this scene?' [Stanislavski] looked surprised and said: '"Emotional states" What is that? I never heard of it.' (Benedetti, 1982: 68)

Stanislavski did not develop a theory of *theatre* but of *acting*. Chekhov, on the other hand, was developing a new form of realist theatre. If Stanislavski had paid more attention to the plays Chekhov wrote and how they worked he might have been able to direct them with the respect they deserve. Then Chekhov might not have had to storm out of the theatre at the premiere of *The Cherry Orchard* in 1904, the last year of his life, claiming that Stanislavski had ruined

---

[1] See the fascinating correspondence between Stanislavski and Stalin in Benedetti, 1991, pp. 345–6.

[2] Stanislavski died before he could give a formal description of his new method and was not able to revise his earlier books. Richard Boleslavsky had worked with Stanislavski in 1908 and then emigrated to the United States. He was unaware of this last phase of Stanislavski's work and founded the American Laboratory Theatre. Among his pupils was Lee Strasberg and under his influence emotional memory became the 'Method'. Strasberg later knew of the new method of physical actions in 1934 and rejected it. The 'Method' reworked the early Stanislavski anyway by the actor taking the text into his own personality and experience rather than working on the given circumstances. See Benedetti, 1982, p. 72 *et seq.*

his play: the same thing he had said about Stanislavski's directing of
The Seagull. I draw the comparison here with Bond. These are the
very things that led to Bond's break with the National Theatre and
the Royal Shakespeare Company. Directors and actors approached
his plays, usually with a Stanislavskian approach to acting, and
ignored the fact that his plays could not be made to work in this
way. The only worse thing to happen to Bond was when his plays
were treated as Brechtian theatre, which Pallitzsch and the Berliner
Ensemble did with *Olly's Prison* (see Bond, 2001: 29).

Bond and theatre

> The future of our species depends on one and only one thing: that the
> Imagination of the adult should be as free as the Imagination of the child.
> Then the adult will Imagine the real – that is, create value in the world of
> facts. In doing this the adult will take responsibility for the world: he or
> she will become part of the map of the world. When adults Imagine the
> real they become human: otherwise they are not Human – then
> Imagination is owned by the state and produced as Ideology, the
> falsehoods behind which are the fairy tales of murderers. And that is the
> history of this time. (Bond, 2000: 101)

This extraordinary and yet ordinary statement of Bond's contains the
essence of his philosophy and the essence of what he is always aiming
to do in his plays. It is extraordinary because he is claiming that the
future of humanity is dependent on one thing, that we start to use our
imagination both to see how the word really is and how we need to
be in it. It is apparently ordinary, because unless we can see the reality
of what is happening in front of our eyes then we are doomed to live
in the nightmare of ideology. His drama works to enable the audience
to be at that crossroads where the human dilemma we are witnessing
is enacted in such a way that we have the chance to see aspects of the
reality of our lives and we have the chance to open ourselves to that
or to confirm ourselves in the belief that the world is as we thought it
was: believing in the fairy tales of murderers.

If Brecht is about distancing the audience from the event to see it
from the outside, from a critical distance, like a scientist examining
a specimen, seeing the individual only in a generalised form, and
Stanislavski is about foregrounding the individual experience before
the social concerns, then Bond is about the audience's *immediate*
confrontation with the relationship of the individual and the social.

Brecht uses the methods described above to put the audience in a relationship to the events where they have, or rather are manipulated into having, the moral high ground 'thinking above the stream' (Brecht: 1978/64: 44). In Bond's plays 'The audience are shown their site by being placed in it – not, as in Brecht, outside it' (Bond, 2000: 11), imagination seeking reason with the audience up to their necks *in* the stream.

> What I try to do in my plays is to speak directly to every individual to make them responsible for their own assessment and involvement in what is being shown – from the individual into the general – not to try and impose a general concept. (Bond, 2004)

Unlike with Brecht, there is no right way to respond to Bond's plays. Each member of the audience has to find his or her own humanness or confirm his or her own corruption. Bond usually does this by moving the play to extreme moments. There is a logic to this. We are so used to the horrors of the world that we can end up not seeing them or 'seeing' them and moving on. 'Our society should be intolerable to us but we accept it and get on' (Bond, 2004). If we could actually hear the cries for food of all the starving children in the world, actually see the hundreds of thousands of faces of children watching their parents die of Aids, personally witness the numbed movements of the millions of displaced people, hear the shouts of all those being tortured, feel the grief of those whose houses have been bombed and whose families have been destroyed, we too might shut ourselves up like Goya, in our own House of the Deaf, covering the walls with paintings, like that of *Saturn Eating his Son*.[1] That is, drawing the monsters, the aggressors, who dehumanise us. This is why Bond puts capitalism in the dock, not individuals. 'How to be human in an inhuman society? – that is the question' (Bond, 2000: 97). His plays seek to confront us with that moment. He does not show us a million children crying but just one; the million are in the one. He exposes

---

[1] Goya (1746–1828) was a Spanish artist who could not turn his eye away from the reality of what he saw. His paintings of royalty show 'warts and all'. In later life he painted his own direct vision of the sufferings in the world. *Saturn Eating his Son* is one of these pictures, one of fourteen he painted while he lived in a house which had been called *Quinta del Sordo* (Deaf Man's House) before he bought it. It is a coincidence that he was himself profoundly deaf when he lived there (although it may have been an ironic choice on his part). He covered the walls of his house with these paintings. This one was in the dining room.

what we are responsible for by being members of a society. Bond is interested in the audience as potential aggressors who are also open to the temptation of revenge. The killing in *Saved* can be seen as a revenge killing. Bond puts us in the extreme moment so we can't 'accept it and get on'. His extreme always concerns the particular which contains the whole: the one crying baby which contains all crying babies. We have, at least, to face that moment and even if we walk out of the theatre as people did at the first production of *Saved*, then at least they take that image with them. They have not been able to pass it by. The extreme does not necessarily entail the act of violence itself. In Bond's play *Coffee*, the soldiers drink coffee while they 'work': their 'job' it is to massacre people. The soldiers are on one side of a ravine, their victims are forced to walk along a ledge on the opposite side. This is based on the massacre of Jews at Babi Yar. Over 33,000 were killed in two days. The extreme is in the drinking of the coffee while they are killing or rather in the throwing away of the coffee in disgust because they thought they had finished their day's 'work'. Instead they have to stop their break and go back to 'work'. In a modern film we would see half an hour of people being shot: Bond exposes the moment by one person throwing the coffee away in exasperation. The question we are faced with in the audience is: What would I do? Not what do I think I would do or what would I like to do – but what *would* I do, in that situation? Why does Bond put us in the extreme moment and what devices has he developed – completely different to Brecht's form of theatre?

Before we can begin to look at the drama devices he has developed over the years, it is essential to grasp what all these are focused on: Bond's theory of human creativity, the creativity of the newborn child. Bond has an original and important new approach to the very early, pre-linguistic, formative period of the life of every human being. Here, for the only time in our lives, as a baby, we are free of ideology. We strive to be at home in the world. We are comfortable with warmth and food and scream with rage if these are denied us. 'Nothing else has the dignity of a crying child' (Bond, 2003: 121). The baby strives for what we will later call justice. The baby is conscious but does not yet have a 'self'. Bond uses the technical term 'neonate' to describe the baby. He has written about this state and its importance at length and in detail. Here he summarises the main points:

The neonate is conscious but not self-conscious. It does not yet have a self that distinguishes between self and other people. Instead its consciousness is coterminous with everything – it *is* the universe. We have to imagine this radical state and not read our later self into it. The neonate cannot know that events outside it *are* outside because it does not have a concept of 'outside'. It will know the events but not their 'site'. Some idea of this can be grasped if we think of a clock that does not know it is telling the time. This is like the neonate before it has a self but is instead an oceanic consciousness in infinity and eternity. There comes a point when it becomes conscious that (to pursue the analogy) it is telling the time. How does this happen? Obviously when someone asks it what the time is – that is, when the neonate becomes aware that there is a being outside itself which is imposing *its* needs on *it*. That is the event – the 'singularity' – in which the neonate creates its *self*, and becomes a being which is active in our world. This singularity can be compared with the way in which all humans thought the world was flat till science found it is round. Then everything changed. But the change is even more fundamental when the neonate learns it is not the universe but that there is a world objectively outside it. That is the moment it creates a self. This process becomes the structure of drama and the creation of the self is the basis of all later creativity. We are the dramatic species.

When the neonate 'was' everything, all it did – *whatever* it did – was its way of seeking to be at home in the universe (that is in and with itself). It is radically innocent. Later, in the adult objective world, this becomes the need for justice. The neonate was responsible for 'justice' in its self-universe. But when it enters the outside world it finds, for reasons some of which are naturally determined and some of which we may call historically contingent, that society is unjust. But the neonate has by then neurologically structured in its brain its imperative to seek justice. That is the human imperative and it may be disremembered but not forgotten. So in unjust society the self is divided against the self. Because of this things turn into their opposites, the same motive producing opposite effects. In this way the structural need for justice may be corrupted into the desire for revenge. And the greatest paradox of all is that the neonate's egocentricity is the only possible basis for human altruism. Humanness is not an ideal or aspiration or one instinct among others – it is a rational imperative ineradicably structured in our mind. We are human *a priori*. Our genes make humanness possible but it cannot be reduced to them. Instead, what determines humanness is how consciousness appears to itself. This is the way the teeming paradoxes of drama are created and drama becomes the 'consciousness' of history. (Bond, 2008d)

It is only at this first, pre-ideological stage that the human is face-to-face with objective reality, with no intervening screen of ideology. It will never be there again. Bond's whole work as a playwright is to take us as close to objective reality as possible: how the world really is, not how we are told it is. He does this not by *telling us* of the reality, as Brecht does, but *taking us there*, to the self-site and finding the drama devices that will connect with our fundamental impulse to humanness, our Radical Innocence.

While the primary concern for both Brecht and Bond is to expose the ideology in which we are trapped, Brecht does this by saying to the audience, open your eyes wider. They both use objects and images of human dilemmas but Brecht attempts to manipulate the audience away from any immediate empathetic relationship with the characters in the play, removing them from the play's site and their own site and putting them back firmly on the social site which is blinding them anyway. Bond says this is like asking the blind to open their eyes wider and look more closely so they can see what is happening, or as he puts it, 'this is like asking the mad to understand they are mad, as useful as asking the eyes to listen' (Bond, 2000: 144). As Belsay states in the quote I have used earlier, 'consciousness is not the origin of the language we speak and images we recognize, so much as the product of the meanings we learn and reproduce.' What is needed, according to Bond, is a method of getting round behind the audience's ideological eyes and finding ways to resonate with their own, pre-ideological eyes, their Radical Innocence. The rage of the radical innocent, seeking to be at home in the world, is heard all through Scene Four of *Saved*. Again, 'Nothing else has the dignity of a crying child.' Whereas Brecht tries to instruct the audience how they should see things, for Bond, drama cannot teach: 'Drama cannot instruct, it confronts, perplexes and intrigues imagination into recreating reality' (Bond, 1995: xxxiv).

The concept of Site

Throughout his plays Bond builds in situations, encounters, events, where the site of change is to be found. At these moments, we in the audience have to meet these events as individuals: these moments become the site of our own humanness. We are given the chance to see our situation more clearly or we can turn away from this understanding. Site is a fundamental concept in Bondian drama (see Bond, 2000: 10–19).

Sites are opportunities for the actors and director to find ways to expose the social forces that are working on the characters in the play through a direct connection between that critical moment and the experience of the audience. The characters are placed in the wider Site of the play. This Site is their total, objective situation: it is the places and the events where humanness is created or undermined. But the Site is also subjective because it always includes the 'self' (created in the way Bond describes) and so the self of the audience is included in the Site created on stage. In drama, whatever happens on stage happens also in the self of the audience. They are not mere spectators. This is because the self must always seek meaning – this is simply the result of the way in which the self is created by the early infant. The audience is not just 'on stage', they *are* in a sense the stage. This accounts for the particular nature of the reaction that may be found to Bond's plays. It is the difference between theatre and drama, acting and enacting. What is the general Site of the characters in *Saved*? It is the world of dead-end jobs and confining walls that stifle any chance of human creativity as soon as it is born. The working class are not human beings, they are 'hands' to be used to make profit for others by working, or mouths to make profit by useless consuming. They are turned into commodities. The stultifying drabness of daily life inhibits human expressions of love and sex; smothers family life; turns the possibility of friendship into routinised displays of 'manhood'. The army prepares young people to be objects at the disposal of dominant class forces, to kill on demand without feelings and the law restores the *status quo ante*, the oppressive social order. In total, it destroys the possibility of a child being at home in the world, literally as well as metaphorically. This is the social site and the actors are on that site in the play, as we are in our lives outside the theatre. However, their responsibility is to enable the audience to relate to that site, through the actions and objects, in such a way that we, the audience, on our self-site, the site of the imagination, can face ourselves in those moments where the play's centre is engaged.

The characters' Sites are also particularised at various stages as part of the larger picture: in a park, that pretence at countryside for the working class to 'relax' in by boating or fishing; in a café, where egg and chips is a feast for a released prisoner; in a front room which must do as dining room, 'lounge' and dressing room, dominated by the messages of the media on a TV that doesn't work; in a police cell so that 'justice' may be meted out. However, in the theatre, it must also be the Site of the audience's imagination. The aim of the whole group of creative artists, the playwright, actors, director, stage designer and all those engaged in the creation of the work of art, is to engage with the audience's Radical Innocence so that they are not just being entertained but their emotions, especially empathy, and thinking are focused closely on minute details, through the use of objects, gesture, posture, in fact all the means at the disposal of the actor to set up a tension, contradiction, to be resolved. These are also Sites where the forces acting to dehumanise us are exposed. How did a 'game' turn into a murder with the stoning of a baby? How did the father of the child come to get involved in killing his own son? Primarily the question is not what does this say about the characters but what does this say about the society that we tolerate by living in it? What does it say about us and where do we stand in relation to this? We can't just condemn it, as we also condone such a society, and if we do so we are in effect the impresarios of the infanticide. The whole approach to the play has to focus on enabling this sort of engagement with the audience.

Approaching the directing and acting of Bond's plays

How, then, should director and actors approach a Bond play? Bond suggests that every play worthy of the name has a centre and even a central line. Each character will say or paraphrase the central line at least once. The whole play needs to be approached to expose and explore this centre. Each situation in the play analyses the central situation and develops its meaning. It is like using building blocks to build a structure. This in itself places an obligation on directors of the plays. If the centre is not used in this way the story collapses into meaninglessness because the usual ideological underpinnings are not there to support any alternative.

What is the centre of *Saved*? And even more interesting, what might be the central line? I think Bond would not be didactic here. This would depend on the creative artists working on the play, but it would have to be a possible reading of the play. In *Saved* the centre is surely a community of people with no understanding of their lives; people who have not been able to acquire the tools to understand themselves and their lives. Like so many people, they live in a moral vacuum; a 'life' that threatens to smother their humanness completely. Bond writes 'in the paradoxes of drama, the young men kill the baby as a means of asserting their self-respect. If this seems an outrageous suggestion, it should be even more outrageous that it is the paradoxical truth of our society' (Bond, 2008d). Len is the only person actively fighting against this way of life. Of course, Len does not understand what he is doing, but at least he is working towards understanding. The central line is even more interesting. Is it the several times repeated 'This is the life', or Pam's 'Yer can't call it living', or Len's 'No one tells yer anything really', or many other possibilities? There is not a definitive answer here. The pursuit would be to open up the chosen centre.

What then are the tools that enable this to happen? Fundamental to this process is the use of Objects, the Drama Event (formerly Theatre Event), Acting the Invisible Object, Accident Time and the Extreme, all evoking imagination to seek reason. It is worth remembering it took some thirty years after people first saw the Berliner Ensemble in London in the mid-1950s before some of Brecht's terminology, alienation effect, the not-but, montage and *gestus*, became properly understood and common currency. Like Brecht, Bond has spent a large part of his life in exile, not living in another country but working in La Colline, a part of the National Theatre in France, in exile from mainstream British theatre. The only UK theatre company to give him a base to try out his plays and theatre form has been Big Brum Theatre in Education company in Birmingham.[1] This has meant his plays and the necessary theory to accompany these plays are just not widely enough known, which leaves a great gap in modern drama in this country. So let us take a look at some of Bond's terminology.

Bond's drama devices

A key device for getting round behind ideological eyes is Bond's different use of objects. 'If no objects, no drama' (Bond, 1998b). He chooses objects that are ideologically neutral or, where the ideological content is marked, it can be deconstructed and turned against itself. A spoon, for example, is usually ideologically neutral, as is a packet of crisps. A crown, on the other hand, is ideologically loaded with implications. However, the spoon or the packet of

[1] See artistic director Chris Cooper's account of rehearsing several of the plays Bond wrote for them in Cooper (2005). He is using the theory and it is most useful to see the practical struggle to realise Bondian theatre.

crisps can be given value in the course of the play. In Bond's play for Big Brum, *The Balancing Act*, the crisps appear or are referred to, some forty times. When they first appear they are just a snack. Then they are used to create an image of humanity ending, like people sinking through the sea because their ship has sunk, but they don't know they are dead, and Viv, the young woman in the play, empties the packet of crisps on to the floor to show how they sank. The crisps have been cathexed, to use Bond's term for this process. They have been given a value at that moment in the play. Her boyfriend tells her she is daft and scoops them up and puts them back in the packet. They are decathexed. They become just crisps again. In *Saved*, for example, some of the ideologically neutral objects used are a teapot, a worm being baited up for fishing, the *Radio Times*, a bread knife, just to look at a few of the objects around which each scene of *Saved* is constructed.

It is the teapot which is suddenly given value (cathexed) in the row between Harry and Mary because she had her skirt up for Len to mend her stocking. It is not the wedding ring which is flung back at her husband but the teapot, a wedding present given to her twenty-three years before, which is smashed over his head. Because it was a wedding present, it forms a regular point of Mary and Harry's struggle for ownership and control in their relationship. There is something bathetic about a teapot holding the promise of domestic bliss together – the endless cups of tea it would pour in their idyllic life together. It holds such a limited vision of married life: the limited expectations society put on their lives, just as it is a disappearing *Radio Times* that Pam can use as a weapon against Len.

In Bond's plays there is usually a strong, clear story line as opposed to Brecht's notion of episodes and montage, which don't need to be connected by story line. However, the story is not the drama. The way the play is structured provides opportunities for theatre/drama events to deconstruct the story. 'The TE [Theatre Event he now calls a Drama Event] takes an action which the audience thinks it understands and then stages it in such a way that its meaning is changed' (Bond, 2004). Some of the TEs are written into the play, such as the cracking of the teapot and others have to be found by the director and actors. Many are indicated in the text. The breaking off of the chair leg, Len's biting off of the thread, Pam's rubbing of her hair, the losing of the needle and so on. The one thing that only the actor can find is what Bond calls the

Invisible Object. This is perhaps usefully thought of as making what is normally invisible, visible: the opaqueness of ideology stripped away, what is objectively there made clear.

This is why the actors are the most important resource for Bond. 'I don't think writing is the most important part of theatre – acting is – writers can only do so much – actors can do more if they understand what is written' (Bond, 2004). Play the play, not the character, is the most important advice that Bond would give an actor. The stage directions are written very carefully to open up the social meaning of the situation. Following these carefully will lead to the play's centre. This leads to enacting, not acting. As I have explained, Bond says that enactment is an event that takes place not just on the stage but in the self of the audience and therefore it changes stage fiction into audience reality. It uses and exposes the unjust social forces with which the audience's own lives are entangled and with which they may compromise in order to survive. When Bond was working with the actors on the recent production of *Saved* at the Abbey Theatre, Dublin, they (some of the actors and Bond) were walking over the River Liffy and saw a beggar holding out his hand with head down and Bond suggested to the actor playing Mary that that was how she could hold the teapot after it was cracked. It suggests many layers of meaning: there is nothing left; she is helpless; *she* is empty; she has given up; she is in despair; her dreams were false and so on. The actor has to find the way to do this, to make the moment resonate with significance, to make what was invisible, the objective reality, visible.

Bond insists 'only the actor may create this…[creating] expressions of gesture, posture, movement, voice […] his perception or reaction to the event' (Bond, 2006). And again Bond insists this is different to a Brechtian approach:

> [This is] a difference I would have with Brecht – he'd want to generalise – a gesture – but I think it is the particular uniqueness of gesture that actually tells you they are part of humanness. The eye is not stupid – the eye sees socially – dramatic truth comes out of facing the paradox of a situation […] human truth has value in it – different to linear truth. (Bond, 2004)

This is where the emotional involvement of the actors is important. Not finding the emotion from a study of the character and applying it to the situation, but extracting it from the situation. Play the situation, not the character.

As Bond began to develop a vocabulary for what he found he was doing, the places where DEs can be found also become clearer. A later example of a DE, that requires the actor finding the way of acting the Invisible Object, is the example Bond writes about in one of his War Plays, *Red, Black and Ignorant* (Bond, 1998a: 313–16). The mother's son has been sent into the street in which his family is still living to kill a civilian. There are only two families left living in the street. The mother is helping her son get ready to go out and kill someone from the other family. She helps him into his jacket, hands him his helmet and gun, all the while talking like a mother getting her son ready to go out on any normal day. 'I'll help you as I did when you were a child.' Bond suggested, in one production, that the soldier's flak jacket might be propped up beside him, suggesting the image of a soldier already dead, so when she helps him on with it she is helping him to take death out into the streets with him. She is his enemy. The aim here is to evoke imagination to seek reason – how far do we as parents, when we are getting our own children ready to go to school, take our part in preparing them to accept the culture they are growing up in, preparing them to take orders, preparing them for the day when they may come back to kill us. The way the mother helps the son get ready necessitates the actor finding the Invisible Object.

Bondian drama in practice

In a workshop Bond gave about TEs (Bond, 1998b), he used scenes from *Eleven Vests*, a play he wrote for Big Brum Theatre in Education company. It is a play about a schoolboy (called the Student throughout the play, even when he is a soldier), who in the first half of the play is confronted by authority, in the form of a head teacher, who is accusing him of 'destructive' behaviour: defacing a book, tearing a pupil's blazer and so on. In the end, the student stabs and kills the head teacher. In the second half of the play we see the student in the army being taught how to bayonet someone to death. Later again, he is on patrol with another soldier and they capture ten enemy soldiers who have hung out their tee-shirts (the vests of the title) on the side of a tower, as a sign of surrender. An eleventh, not knowing the others have surrendered, fires from the tower and kills the student's fellow soldier. The 'enemy' soldiers, who have surrendered, shout to him, the eleventh soldier, to surrender also. He does so and goes down on his knees in front of the student. The student goes to the shot fellow soldier to check his condition. He is dead. The words given to him in the text are, 'Bastard. You bastard', which he addresses to the eleventh enemy soldier. Bond asked those attending the workshop, if this is personal or professional language, a question he had been asking of the workshop audience as Big Brum actors re-created the whole scene. Many said it was personal. Bond assured them that every line in the scene is professional including 'Bastard. You bastard.' (It is worth noting that there is no exclamation mark after either 'bastard'.) This is not a buddy movie which can obscure what war is really about: politics carried on by other means.

He demonstrated how the director and the actors could find the DE here. He put an identity tag round the dead soldier's neck and got the student, after checking for a pulse, to pull off the identity tag. His 'buddy' really is, objectively, also a number. Bond got the actor to say the line quite quietly, in an unbelieving way. This wasn't supposed to happen. It broke the Geneva Convention and the rules of engagement. Once they had surrendered, hostilities were supposed to be over. Neither side should attempt to kill the other. All the while, the intercom crackles, attempting to make contact. It is the voice of authority, the officer directing the 'operation'. Two human beings face each other, with no language in common, each led by their respective voices of authority to kill the other. The student, ignoring the voice of his authority, bayonets the soldier who has surrendered. He wipes the blood off the bayonet with the eleventh vest. Then an extraordinary moment occurs, the bayoneted soldier, not yet dead, sits up and crawls towards the student. He also picks up the tee-shirt and wipes his own blood off the bayonet, all the while saying things in his own language. The soldier's act is militarily harmless – but paradoxically its strangeness works on the student as if he had been threatened with a gun. He panics and bayonets the soldier again – this time to death. Then the paradox begins to have a different, more radical effect. The student becomes obsessed with trying to understand what the soldier had said. Over and over again he repeats the strange words.

When some French students asked Bond what the words meant he said he didn't know – he had made up a stage language. It is for the audience to say what the soldier meant. It is also up to the actor to use the event to create the invisible object – in the way he tries to repeat the strange words, or perhaps in some other way the actor chooses. In the extreme moment the actor shows the student's search for meaning. The Invisible Object becomes an image of Radical Innocence. For the first time in his life, as far as we know it, the student is reaching out for the meaning of the event, no matter in how limited a fashion. Here, the audience are impelled into the Gap, the term Bond uses for the space between us and Nothingness. This gap is usually occupied by authority and its ideology, a state which Bond describes as 'the owning of nothingness'. But in the extreme, drama shows an event which ideology cannot adequately explain, except with empty rhetoric – instead the audience themselves are directly confronted with Nothingness. This happens in Accident Time and in it we must find or dismiss our humanness. It is where the stranglehold of ideology is broken or we escape into reaction and corruption. If it is into corruption, then we become the voice of ideology.

Bond also points out that any play, worthy of being a play, can be DE'd (made into a Drama Event). An example he gives is from *Hedda Gabler* by Ibsen. Towards the end of the play, Hedda has purloined the manuscript of her one time platonic lover. He is distraught at the loss of his manuscript, the only copy of his life's work. It is a masterpiece and concerns the course of the future of humanity. She burns it saying the lines, 'Now I am burning your child, Thea.' A Stanislavskian interpretation would be to find the jealousy inside the actress that she could relate to and would show it as a personal moment. In one contemporary production that Bond saw, the actress first 'dashed across the room and overturned a table. The cheap melodramatics of our present theatre' (Bond, 2002). Bond suggests that to find the DE the actress could start to throw the sheets into the fire and then as she is doing so, read a page and want to read on but find she has thrown the next page on to the fire. She retrieves it but it is burning. The skill of the actor here would be to find the Invisible Object, the reflection of bombed cities or crematoria: burning the book has consequences for humanity, and this would be first shown in the sudden inexorable re-emergence of humanness in Hedda Gabler. If she burns her fingers without noticing it to start with, because she is suddenly so intent, caught up in really reading for the first time what she is destroying, then you might have the burning cities and crematoria.

If we return to the question posed earlier, as to why there are such intricate stage directions for Len in the final scene where he is mending the chair, it should now be possible to bring the devices to bear on this scene. This should enable me to substantiate my earlier claim that all the major components of Bond's drama were there from the beginning. The Site is the 'living' room, where the messengers of this living death are present: the promise of escape to another life through Harry's football pools, the *Radio Times* for Pam and Mary. The mending of the chair in the silence of the room is, I would suggest, the main Drama Event of the play. It continues the story of this 'family' but chooses an event where the story can be deconstructed. Finding the Invisible Object here is the particular way these 'poses' are found and held. This entails following the stage directions carefully. This is the site that is being excavated. There is an object, the chair, an ordinary everyday object, but one that has already been cathexed with value/meaning earlier in the play. Possibly it stopped Harry from striking Mary, but involved breaking up the home. Now it is being repaired. To start with there are two bangs off stage, subliminally this might suggest Len committing suicide. But why the intricate stage directions for trying to mend the chair? Bond says he took the poses from Michelangelo sculptures. In a sense, they suggest heroic poses or rather humanly dignified poses. Len might look exhausted or somewhat despairing but it is not the exhaustion or despair of Mary and Harry. He has not been beaten down into submission. In the silence of the room, in its frightening deadness, he still struggles on: it is like Michelangelo's late statues of slaves crawling out of the stone in which they are carved. 'The IO [Invisible Object] is shown when humanness is created in the choice made in the confrontation between humanness and corruption or emptiness' (Bond, 2006). When this connects with the audience it creates what Bond calls Accident Time. 'It does not offer the security of escape but compels involvement: the spectator is drawn into the event. It is a moment of absolute concentration' (ibid.). Bond draws this notion from the way the mind goes into slow motion when the body is in danger. Time appears to slow down to give the mind time to work. In Accident Time, the audience enters the Gap, the place where ideology is unable to give us the answers, where without this device we might just see a 'normal' working-class family at peace with itself: this would be the Nothingness owned by the culture. It is the area where the connection with Radical Innocence is sought. We, the audience, have to create or deny our humanness. In this final scene we are faced with taking responsibility for our lives, for our society, for our world.

Opening up the scene in the way described above is not acting but enacting in Bond's terminology. It makes it possible to see what is actually, objectively, going on. In this sense, it is not a question of concentrating on the inner motivations of the character but of playing the character on the site of the play. Don't play the character, play the play, is the regular advice he gives. Stop acting, is his advice to actors. He means start enacting: start to lay bare the processes which enable, or deprive us of, our humanity.

In the first German production of *Saved* the actress playing Mary insisted on 'banging' the tablecloth on the table as she cleared up – snapping it in the air. She said that her character was angry and this is what she would do. She was playing the character and not the play. The director wanted to play a radio throughout the scene. It was a Brechtian device. Bond insisted on the silence.

To summarise simplistically: Brecht is focused on the social, the objective, through reason; Stanislavski is focused on the subjective, the personal, through character; Bond focuses the subjective and the objective, the character, the personal, in the social, through evoking the imagination to seek reason. Brecht works to *alienate* the audience through his theatre devices, montage, the not-but, the *gestus* and so on. These see the human being as some sort of reasoning machine. Bond works to draw in the audience, to *confront* us through his devices, the Extreme, the Drama Event, Accident Time, cathexing and decathexing objects, the Invisible Object and so on. These see the human individual as someone who can be, has to be, creatively responsible for him- or herself and the rest of humanity: humanity Radically Innocent, embodying the human imperative to seek justice. Brecht's theatre is a theatre for the scientific age, the present 'Age of Reason'; Stanislavski's, via the Method, is a theatre for capitalism; what Bond is seeking to create is a theatre of the people, a public theatre.

Bond and Marxism

Earlier, I suggested that it could be argued that Brecht was never really a Marxist. By this I meant that he remained a mechanical materialist.[1] He learned basic tenets of Marxist theory which he used to analyse society around him. He exposes his linear thinking by referring to Marxism as 'the ideology of order and reason' (Fuegi, 1987: 48). He remained a Stalinist all his life. To wit his awful, servile comment on the terrible Moscow Trials, where a whole generation of revolutionaries were wiped out by Stalin, indicted in farcical trials with falsified evidence, all to tighten his stranglehold over the Party apparatus: 'Stalin may have served the people by removing the enemies in the [Party], but he hasn't proved it' (quoted in Willett, 1998). Brecht meant that during the trials not enough evidence had been produced to show their guilt clearly. To paraphrase Trotsky, there is a river of blood between Stalinism and Marxism. Brecht's lack of empathy in his own dealings, his abysmal treatment of women (Fuegi, 1987: 50), his determination to manipulate for himself the allocation of by far the greatest amount of money in any contract, even to the point of demeaning and cutting out collaborators (which caused a long-standing embitterment between Weil and Brecht, for example; Fuegi, 1987: 60), all this linear thinking in his dealings, mark out the territory of the deep divisions between Brecht's and Bond's Marxism.

The essential difference between Brecht's claimed Marxism and Bond's Marxism is that Bond is searching for a living Marxism, imbued with human value. 'I am a strict materialist but what does that mean in human terms?' (Bond, 2008a). And again, we find in Bond, quoting Marx, 'Not social consciousness determines their being but their social being determines their consciousness. I have no problem with that – really that's what I'm saying but trying to say how does it come about – the problem for me is *yes* – but how does it come about?' (Bond, 2004). His answer is to be found in the ineluctable drive of human beings to create their own humanness: the drive for justice, meaning the search for and creation of human values. Here the imagination is key for Bond. It is the human ability to be able to release ourselves from the hold of the immediate that brings the greatest opportunities and the greatest problems. However,

---

[1] I mean this in the same way that Richard Dawkins is locked into mechanical materialism. We are simply the product of our 'selfish genes'. Contrast this with Steven Rose's approach in his book *Lifelines: Biology, Freedom, Determinism* and his *Lifelines: Beyond the Gene* to find a dialectical materialist at work. Likewise with Lewontin's (with Rose and Kamin) *Not in Our Genes: Biology, Ideology and Human Nature* and Lewontin and Levin's *Biology Under the Influence: Dialectical Essays on the Co-evolution of Nature and Society.*

the imagination, the seeking for meaning, the self-consciousness that is synonymous with imagination, the imagination that seeks reason, is what is dramatised in Bond's plays. 'We would be human – all our acts would be human – if the childhood autonomy of imagination extended into adulthood' (Bond, 1995: xxxi). What Bond seeks is the Promethean Radical Innocence integrated with, but not subdued by, later experience – what he calls 'the weight of the world'. In a recent interview with Bond he affirmed that he is not a structuralist, definitely not a poststructuralist but more a post-poststructuralist[1] and that the 'logic of humanness is absolutely opposed to postmodernism' (Bond, 2008a). 'I am a dialectical materialist in the sense I shall try to make clear' (Bond, 2008b). What he goes on to make clear is this ineluctable drive for human value that has to permeate all we do. For Bond, the dialectical is the search for the way in which each human has to create his or her own humanness. It can never be a dogma as it was for Brecht.

Saved and censorship[2]

> [a] political furore [...] erupted over the Royal Court's production in November 1965 of Edward Bond's *Saved*. No other play this century posed such pressing, practical problems for a government. The Home Secretary, Lord Chancellor, the Attorney-General, Director of Public Prosecutions and various law officers were all involved. (De Jongh, 2001: 214)

Censorship in the theatre started in 1543, under Henry VIII, mainly with an anti-Catholic purpose. The Puritans later closed the theatres, which were re-opened under the Restoration of Charles II. The freedom of expression which then existed for a short time ended with a new Stage Licensing Act. This Act of

---

[1] Interviewer: 'I want to write that you are not a poststructuralist'; Bond: 'I'm sure that is absolutely right' (Bond, 2008a). Structuralism is a way of examining language, society, behaviour etc. to find the patterns/rules by which they are structured. Its weakness is to study phenomena in isolation and synchronically (examining areas at one specific time, often only the present), not diachronically (examining areas over a period of time in history). For poststructuralism see p. xxvii above. Postmodernism: 'Incredulity towards meta-narratives [overarching discourses, such as fascism, communism etc.]' (Lyotard). Dialectical materialism is the opposite of mechanical materialism where human beings are trapped as objects shaped by material forces. The dialectical for Bond is the active, revolutionising consciousness of the human subject.

[2] I have drawn heavily in this section on de Jongh's excellent book (2001).

1737, amended in 1752, 1755 and by the Theatre Regulation Act of 1843, gave the Lord Chamberlain[1] complete authority over which plays could be performed and what should be cut out. It was no accident that this authority came to the Lord Chamberlain rather than to a committee of the government. It meant the state had direct control over what was seen in the theatres. Under the pretence of preserving 'good taste', the main aim was to censor political criticism of the crown and government and any criticism of friendly sovereigns or powers (De Jongh, 2001: pp. 21–2). In 1938, Terence Rattigan submitted *Follow My Leader*, a light play satirising the German leaders in a thinly disguised form. It caused the censor no end of problems. About the play he wrote, 'The dictator is a puppet which Hitler is not. The Field Marshal is a fool which Goering is not. The propaganda minister is inefficient which Goebbels is not' (ibid., p. 143). It was sent to the German Embassy by the Lord Chamberlain's Office. The German Embassy replied that they thought it would not be helpful to Anglo-German relations, this at a time when the Nazis were massed on the border of Poland ready to invade. The play was refused permission to be performed. A year later war was declared and the play was given a licence.

In 1891, Ibsen had given the censors apoplexy. The Chief Examiner of plays, E. F. Smyth-Pigott, wrote:

> Do not come to me with Ibsen. [...] I have studied Ibsen's plays pretty carefully [...] All the characters [...] appear to be morally deranged. All the heroines are dissatisfied spinsters who look on marriage as a monopoly, or dissatisfied married women in a chronic state of rebellion not only against the conditions which nature has imposed on their sex, but against all the duties and obligations of mothers and wives; and as for the men they are all rascals or imbeciles.
> (Ibid., pp. 30–1)

---

[1] The Lord Chamberlain is a senior member of the Queen's household. He is responsible for organising all court functions, e.g. royal marriages. He is always a peer and a member of the Privy Council. (The Privy Council is presided over by the Queen and is a potential power structure inside the formal state. It has the power to dissolve Parliament when it is time for an election and also in the case of a national emergency. At such a time Parliament could be dissolved and the country run by the Privy Council.) The Lord Chamberlain, from 1755 to 1968, was also responsible for the licensing and censorship of all plays.

Was there ever better evidence for the need for playwrights who would challenge the social order and ruling ideology?

When Smyth-Pigott retired, his place was taken by Alexander Redford, a retired bank manager. When asked in 1909 by what criteria he judged plays, he replied, 'I have no critical view of plays. I simply have to maintain standards' (ibid., p. 31). Strindberg's *Miss Julie* fared no better. 'I have been at some pains to wade through this filthy piece,' wrote a seventy-three-year-old member of the Advisory Board, Sir Johnston Forbes-Robertson (ibid., p. 67). Until 1958, the Lord Chamberlain maintained a total ban on the discussion or depiction of homosexuality on the stage. The long list of playwrights who had their plays censored or banned included: Tennessee Williams, Jean Genet, Samuel Beckett, Arthur Miller, Noël Coward and, of course, Edward Bond.

However, after the Second World War, social conditions were changing. The context was developing where censorship would be tolerated less and less. During the war there had been far greater mixing of classes and after the war a consumer society was developing, rock and roll was on the agenda; attitudes to sex were changing; establishment figures were less symbols of authority and more figures of fun. The loss of Empire continued and England had less and less status as a world power. The scene was set for a severe challenge to theatre censorship and this came from Edward Bond.

In 1965 Bond was one of the new young playwrights at the Royal Court Theatre. Bill Gaskill had just taken over from George Devine as artistic director. He found a copy of *Saved* in Devine's drawer, where it had lain for a year or so, and immediately decided to put it on. The play, of course, had to go to the Lord Chamberlain's Office to be approved. At the end of June 1965, Charles Heriot, the Chief Examiner of Plays, sent his report to Lord Cobbold, the Lord Chamberlain. He described *Saved* as 'A revolting amateur play [...] the writing is vile and the conception worse' (De Jongh, 2001: 215). However he suggested it be given a licence. Interestingly, this advice was ignored. The play was then sent from one person to another to take advice before a decision was given. The person in charge of the Office, the Comptroller, was at that time Lieutenant-Colonel Sir Eric Penn and he sent the script to Terence Nugent, the recently retired Comptroller. His response was swift and clear. 'I've read this revolting play which

certainly ought not to be shown on any stage' (ibid., p.171).[1]
Finally, a letter was sent to the Royal Court listing four pages of
cuts. Examples of these cuts included, 'arse', 'bugger', 'get stuffed',
'crap', 'piss off', and 'shag'; 'The couple must not lie down on the
couch so that one is on top of the other', and 'There must be no
indecent business with the balloon'. Again, 'Pam must not have
unbuttoned too far. Pam must not undo Len's belt.' And so the list
went on and on. This included cutting the whole of Scene Six, the
stoning of the baby scene, and the scene with Len mending Mary's
stocking. George Devine suggested cutting the play, 'Swallow pride
and re-invent' (ibid., p. 216). Bond refused to cut or alter a single
word. Gaskill decided to give it a club run with a members-only
audience. The Lord Chamberlain asked the Director of Public
Prosecutions if he could take court proceedings. This would test if
an unlicensed play could be shown to members-only club
audiences. Meanwhile the play opened to an onslaught from the
critics.

> It may not be the feeblest thing I have seen on any stage, but it is certainly
> the nastiest, and contains perhaps the most horrid scene in the
> contemporary theatre. (Even as I write that hedging 'perhaps' I delete it:
> nobody can hedge about *Saved*.) (Trewin in the *Illustrated London News*,
> 13 November 1965)[2]

> Terror and horror in the theatre can offer release and cleansing. *Saved*
> would have left me feeling soiled and dirty but for its eventual nullity.
> (*Sun*, 4 November 1965)

> The writing itself, with its self-admiring jokes and gloating approach to
> moments of brutality and erotic humiliation amounts to a systematic
> degradation of the human animal. (Irving Wardle, *The Times*, cited in
> Scharine, 1976: 48)

[1] To give some indication of the level of awareness of these people, the *Saved*
furore was only a few years after the Lord Chamberlain, Lord Scarborough, did
not know what 'crumpet' meant. Brigadier Sir Norman Gwatkin did not know
either and he had to ask. Heriot replied that crumpet was 'a recognised
pseudonym for "the female pudenda"'. When it came to 'screw' in the sexual
sense, this caused as much confusion in the Office. 'I'll screw you in that chair',
in a play called *Tomorrow with Pictures*, was disallowed. Trying to be helpful
they offered that, 'The word nail would be acceptable.'
[2] Except where otherwise indicated, these quotes are to be found in the Edward
Bond Archive at the Victoria and Albert Theatre Museum.

> [...] the characters, who, almost without exception, are foul-mouthed, dirty-minded, illiterate, and barely to be judged on any recognisable human level at all. (Kretzmer in the *Daily Express*, cited in Scharine, 1976: 48)

> Was there ever a psychopathic exercise so lovingly dwelt on as this, spun out with such relish and refinement detail? (J.W. Lambert in the *Sunday Times*)

> People walked out of the performance and there was some calling out from the audience. (*Birmingham Post*, 4 November 1965)

Bond had hate mail – one in red ink to look like blood and one written in excrement. Initially, the reviews kept the audiences away. To their credit, some people came to the play's defence. Laurence Olivier wrote:

> Unfortunately, the extreme horror of the scene [Scene Six] [...] has run away with most dramatic criticism and blinded it to the real qualities shown in the rest of the play, which from time to time achieves astonishing heights of dramatic powers and contains a last scene of which Chekhov himself would have approved. (Olivier, 1965)

Penelope Gilliatt in the *Observer* wrote one of the few intelligent and sympathetic reviews, 'The mime of life-in-death [of the last scene], is the most horrific thing in the play' (Bond Archive). For her pains she received a photo of her own child with her head cut off.

Lord Cobbold, the Lord Chamberlain, pressed for action against the Royal Court and on 14 February 1966, Bill Gaskill, artistic director of the Royal Court, Greville Poke, the English Stage Company's secretary, and Alfred Esdaile, the licensee of the theatre, were hauled before a magistrate's court and charged with presenting a play 'for hire' under Section 15 of the Theatres Act of 1843. Despite eloquent support from the likes of Laurence Olivier, they were found guilty and fined £50 expenses. The worst aspect of the case was that it meant that the loophole of avoiding the censor by giving club performances was now closed. *Saved* was taken off.

Two days later a proposal was made in Parliament to set up a joint committee of both Houses to review the theatre censorship laws. The Lord Chamberlain was on the way out. The committee reported in 1967 and recommended the end of pre-theatre censorship. Before the law could be brought to Parliament, Edward Bond's next play, *Early Morning*, had been banned outright. In

1969, after the demise of the Lord Chamberlain as theatre censor, *Saved* was given a full run at the Royal Court, along with his other plays. Then came the reviews:[1]

> But it is not a vicious play. It is truthful, compassionate and disturbing and reveals Bond as one of Britain's most heavyweight young playwrights. (Robert McDonald, *Scotsman*, 10 November 1969)

> London's most important play [...] Cleverly, even brilliantly produced, there is undoubtedly justification in the claim that it is the most important play to have been seen on the London stage in the last ten years. (*City Press*)

> The most important British playwright to emerge in the 60s. (Ronald Bryden, *Observer*, November 1969)

> What a brilliant play *Saved* is. (Martin Esslin)

> Edward Bond triumphs at the Royal Court season [...] I do not understand why everyone is being so reticent about acclaiming Bond for who he is. Surely, after *Early Morning* there can be no doubt that he is the most important living dramatist. (Peter Fuller, *City Press*, 27 March 1969)

Prior to this many of the critics had had to eat humble pie. A year after he had written his damning review (see above), Irving Wardle had to write:

> This was the biggest mistake of my reviewing career [...] If I hadn't indulged in the sense of outrage, I might have remembered there were plenty of plays from *King Lear* onwards that match or outclass *Saved* in violence. (Cited in de Jongh, 2001: 222)

Even Bond's former local newspaper claimed him for its own.

> Famous playwright was once Hornsey boy. (Headline in *Hornsey Journal*, Bond Archive)

If anyone doubts the lack of perspicacity of many theatre critics, the first reviews of *Saved* provide the evidence. Without doubt if Bond had not stood firm and refused to cut the play, the whole sorry business of stage censorship might have rolled on for some more years. 'Bond's precipitatory role in accelerating the Lord Chamberlain's demise has been overlooked or unappreciated' (De Jongh, 2001: 237).

---

[1] All the following are to be found in the Bond Archive, Victoria and Albert Theatre Museum.

Saved: structure, design and language

> Edward Bond is an artist who uses his art as a prosecuting attorney uses
> his brief: the defendant is the social order; the crime is perversion of the
> innocent; and the evidence is *Saved*. (Scharine, 1976: 81)

All the people in *Saved* live their lives immersed in ideology. It is
the ideology of capitalism. It is the acceptance of 'the daily round,
the common task'; the acceptance of 'He made us high and low'
and we just have to get on with it. Only Len regularly tries to break
out. He is of course mainly immersed in it as well. In fact, all the
language of the play is ideology, except when Len is trying, without
any guidance, to move towards some sort of more human
existence. The young men are struggling against authority in their
limited way, through their banter, their hatred of work and so on
but in the end all this 'resistance' revolves on itself. The play is an
examination of a section of a community who have been given no
means, by the culture in which they have grown up, of questioning
their lives, of gaining a human self-consciousness. Their mistake is
to try to be at home in the society in which they have been born
instead of trying to be at home in the world. Their imaginations
have been distorted to such an extent that Nothingness, to use
Bond's term, the void to be filled by a struggle for a human
existence and a human value system, is owned by the system that
regulates society: capitalism.

To claim that all the language in the play, except some of Len's,
is ideology, must seem an extreme statement. There is no overtly
religious voice preaching the way to live; no extreme political
agenda being pushed anywhere in the play. One of the interesting
dimensions of the construction of the play is that there *are* no
figures of authority, such as the police, teachers or priests. Nor, for
that matter, are there any voices that might be considered as
ameliorating influences on the way they live, such as social
workers, nor those who might offer an alternative vision of the life
they are leading, such as trade union activists. The people are held
in place by ideology, by their way of viewing the world.[1] Getting

---

[1] More and more in contemporary society ideology is enforced by the use of
constraints such as ASBOs (Anti-Social Behaviour Orders). In Bond's play *Born*,
set in the near future, ideology is completely held in place by force. The Len
character in this play is Luke, a uniformed, armed guardian of the state and law
enforcer. Also in this play a baby is killed, this time smashed against the riot

some sort of job, searching for sex, going fishing, getting married, having a baby, growing old in a dead, stultifying marriage, is what happens. Holding everything in place through ideology is the easiest and most successful way of maintaining a class society and a class of compliant workers who will do all the menial jobs required to keep capitalism functioning. The characters speak the words that society has given them.

> PAM. I'm goin' a knit yer a jumper. [...]
> LEN. We'll have a fair little place. I ain' livin' in no blinkin' sty.
>   [...]
> PAM. 'E puts 'er money over the fire every Friday, an' thass all
>   there is.
> (Scene Two)

> MARY. I don't expect yer t'understand at your age, but things don't
>   turn out too bad. There's always someone worse off in the
>   world.
> LEN (*clearing up the polishing things*). Yer can always be that one.
>   [A response typical of Len.] [...]
> MARY. Yer can't stand a girl in a puddle down the back a some ol'
>   alley an' think yer doin' 'er a favour. Yer got yer own room
>   upstairs. That's a nice room. Surprised yer don't use that.
>   I don't mind what goes on, yer know that. As long as yer
>   keep the noise down.
> LEN. Ta.
> MARY. It's in every man. It 'as t'come out.
> (Scene Nine)

They see their life through little platitudes: 'This is the life'; 'What a life'; 'Free country'; 'Yer only live once' and so on.

The young men communicate through crude sex jokes that prevent them from dealing with the reality of their lives. They clutch at some meaning they think they have of how the system works. 'Accidents is legal' (Mike, Scene Three). The older people don't communicate at all except to row and have a fight. 'Don't speak to

shields of the police, literally in front of the mother's face. Luke wants to know what it is like just before you die. He has killed enough people to know what it is like from the outside. He wants to know what happens inside. He wants the mother to tell him and thinks she will know at the moment of the baby's death. It links with Len's desire to know from Fred what it was like to kill the baby.

'em at all. It saves a lot of misunderstanding (Harry, Scene Twelve).
Cigarettes, sweets, fishing, going out looking for girls or to a
football match, boating in the park, watching TV or the radio, are
all minor panaceas, which are supposed to make the grinding round
of work worth it. On television the other day a young woman was
interviewed and asked what it meant to be British. She replied,
'Goin' to work. Getting' paid. Goin' out and getting' drunk – then
goin' to McDonald's.' Not much has changed.

None of the few agents of authority who are referred to in the
play knows how to communicate with members of this
community; they are seen by the young men as people from
another world. They have no language in common. The coroner in
Scene Three thanks Pete for coming and he is paid for attending,
when he has knocked down a child. This is an occasion to hide
from the reality of what has happened through jokes and making
fun of the proceedings. Later, Fred is sentenced to prison by the
law but, interestingly, we do not see the judge or even a police
officer, although a steel door bangs three times, which is much
more effective. Fred being sentenced to jail is as useless as the
Prince's intervention in *Romeo and Juliet*, after Romeo has killed
Mercutio. All the law's intervention leads to is Romeo's
banishment, which directly feeds into causing the double suicide at
the end of the play. Likewise, Fred and the padre have no way of
connecting.

> FRED. This padre 'as me in.
> BARRY. O yeh.
> FRED. Wants t' chat me up. 'E says nothing that comes out a a
> man can be all bad.
> BARRY. Whass that?
> FRED. Then 'e 'ops out an' I 'as a little slash in 'is tea.
> (Scene Ten)

All prison does for Fred is prepare him, as Len says, to finish up
'like some ol' lag, or an' ol' soak' (Scene Twelve).

None of this is intended as an indictment of young people,
neither here nor in the play. It is capitalist society that is in the dock.
None of the people in the play has been given the means to create
human value and that is as true today as it was in the 1960s. Their
imaginations have been distorted away from human values towards
accepting, or rather not questioning, a system that is unjust. This
can only lead to problems, as it does.

This is why Len's struggle to move towards humanness is the evidence of humanness. Len is in every scene of the play. His are the only actions in the play that seek to break the stranglehold of capitalist ideology or, to put the same thing another way, to begin to use the imagination to work for human values. This is true of every scene in the play except for Scene One where he is out purely for himself and initiates an unkind baiting of Pam's father, albeit as a result of his own insecurity. He is of the same section of the community as the other young men. He is by no means perfect. He does not stop the stoning but watches it. He shows little grieving over the murder of the baby,

> LEN. One a them things. Yer can't make too much a it.
> (Scene Nine)

However, he is always asking questions. He has a burning curiosity. He wants to know what it was like in prison; what it was like when Harry was in the war. Later, his curiosity leads him to want to know from Fred what it was like to kill the baby. Len is conscious of mortality and this is an essential part of humanness, it is one of the things that distinguishes Bond's 'humanness' from 'human being' because human beings may act inhumanly. Mortality is unavoidable and in Len it raises the spectre of the waste of human life.

In Scene Four he does not get up to go to the crying baby but we learn later that he will stay because of the child. He believes it may be his. It is important that Len is not perfect. If he had been, it would have let the audience off the hook. The audience would have had a means of escape. You would have been left with a piece of conventional theatre. His imperfection makes his struggle all the more real and admirable. He is always doing small positive things. Some examples of these are offered here. He waits in the park to help Mary with the shopping. He nurses Pam, all the time being abused by her, and brings the baby in to her. He notices that the pram brake is off and puts it on and then goes after Pam to bring her back. In the police cell, he brings in cigarettes for Fred. He tries to offer sympathy to Harry about the baby lost in the war but is ignored. Len brings Pam a cup of tea in the café. He tries to make peace after Mary and Harry's row. He mends the chair. He learns more about society and about himself in the course of the play. He sees through Fred. He realises that he should have acted during the stoning, 'I should a stopped yer'

(Scene Seven). The clearest line in the play that works against the dominant ideology is Len's, 'Fetch me 'ammer' (Scene Thirteen). Bond points out that Nietzsche says 'I philosophise with a hammer' (Bond, 2008a).

It is crucial that Bond's plays are acted, or rather enacted, as they are written: the acting, and therefore the directing, are essential to the play working as intended. The worst thing that can happen to *Saved* would be for it to be acted as though it were a farce about working-class people, taking an Alf Garnett-type approach,[1] albeit with some very dark moments. This would put the audience above the stream. In Brechtian terms, the situations would be viewed from outside, with the audience on higher moral ground. The actors need to *en*act real lives, the enacting meaning that the social forces working in the situation are always the main concern. Then if there is laughter from the audience, it may be at the recognition of the banality of our own lives or that we are just turning away from our responsibility for the society we live in. We are, in fact, all responsible for the society we live in and the injustices it produces. We condone it by being part of it.

It is formally speaking a comedy: a tragi-comedy. The Oedipal dimension does not lead to sexual consummation with the mother figure and although there is a struggle and a knife, the father figure is not killed but has his head smashed open with a teapot. It would need to be acted so that each event illuminates the site of the characters, opening up the objective dimensions that are impelling these people in these situations and confronting the site of the audience. The Site of the audience is their imagination, their ability to question the way things are, for imagination to seek meaning, to seek reason. The play is written in a way that enables this to happen.

A reporter once asked Bond why it was called *Saved*. He replied, 'It's what goalies do. Think about it!' It seems a clear enough answer to me.

---

[1] Alf Garnett was a character in a TV series which patronised and condescended in its portrayal of working-class family life. Garnett's catchphrase was to call his wife 'a silly old moo'.

Structure

It is a play about people living without meaning. Every stage of development in the play explores this and explores 'the gap between the two realities, the subjective self and the objective world' (Bond, 2008c). It looks a deceptively simple play. However, like all Bond's plays it is very carefully structured. Laurence Olivier pointed out that like Shakespeare's *Julius Caesar*, the murder comes in the middle. This makes the play not primarily about a murder but why a murder is inevitable in this sort of society and deals with its aftermath. Olivier also called it a play with a perfect structure. Each scene is constructed around a few objects and the information we need is built neatly into the dialogue. For example, by the time we get to Scene Three, where the young men are spending the lunch hour in the park, we already know that Len has joked that Pam may be pregnant, that her baby brother was bombed, presumably in a pram, in the park during the war, that her parents don't talk, that Harry has a night job and is a non-person, that Pam looks as though she is going in the same direction in life as her mother, even though she would vehemently deny this, that Len and Pam are thinking of getting married, that Len has a positive side, that he is an inveterate questioner and so on. Early in Scene Three we learn that one of the young men has been involved in the death of another child and is on his way to the funeral: all this through one-liners. The play resonates in each stage with earlier developments as it proceeds.

The story is important in Bond's plays. The scenes aren't episodes in a Brechtian sense. Each scene links very clearly with the one before but with gaps in what has happened, which the audience has to fill in. This is done extremely neatly, usually in one apparently casual line. In Scene Two, with 'I still ain' paid me rent this week', we know that Len has moved in. Scene Three gives us a whole sense of the young men who will later murder a baby. In every line we see the gap between their subjective and the objective reality, without anyone directly pointing to it. In Scene Four, simply the baby crying indicates all that has happened since the previous scene and then that Fred has taken Len's place. Pam's 'Did yer see Fred?' in Scene Five, gives us the immediate clue that things have deteriorated even further. Each scene is neatly moved forward in an economic way that does not mislead the audience but that enables them to work out the leap in what has developed.

Bond says that his plays are not commodifiable (Bond, 2008a). By this he means that his plays are written in such a way that they cannot be turned into just entertainment, into a commodity. This, of course, depends on the way it is directed and acted. If the way Bond's theatre needs to work is ignored or not known, then the plays can become commodities. This happened recently with the West End production of *The Sea*. The main actors could not resist putting on a West End performance, instead of playing the play. The theatre critic, Michael Billington, called it 'superbly acted' but dismissed the play, 'I'm not sure the story is strong enough to bear the cosmic weight imposed on it' (Billington, 2008): precisely the wrong way round. However, this sort of acting destroyed, rather than illuminated the play (Bond, 2007). The same would happen with *Saved* if it were played to bring out the comedy. '*Saved* isn't naturalism – naturalism asks what? realism asks why? and the "why" determines the way "what" is shown' (Bond, 1996b: 122). This directly relates to Bond's admiration for ancient Greek theatre where a burgeoning democracy used the theatre to ask questions of itself. 'The Greeks said what is justice? now the detective says who did it?' (Bond, 1996a).

Each scene has a satisfying structure and with great precision and economy enables us to grasp a great deal: (a) about the characters, their relationships and attitudes, and through this, the society that is shaping them; and (b) about the plot development and the opportunities that this provides for us to connect our site with the site of the play. There is no authorial voice and the audience is left rudderless. We have to guide our own boat. A brief look at each of these scenes in turn may be useful at this point. The play is so tightly structured that it would be possible to comment on every line. Each word is needed: there is nothing superfluous. This means that any comment I might make on any of the scenes can only be a partial comment, drawing attention to some of the main features apparent to me.

In **Scene One**, Pam has picked up Len and brought him home (we learn of this in Scene Two). This is the only time we see her so confident and precocious. She needs attention. She is always needy. One can imagine her having been starved of the love that all children need to grow up secure with themselves. Her quick repartee shows she is better equipped than Len to deal with this situation. In fact, he shows himself a novice.

LEN. Give us a shout if I do somethin' yer don't reckon. [...]
PAM. Ow!

LEN. Sh! Keep quiet now.
PAM. Oi!
LEN. Sh!
PAM. Yer told me t'shout.

They are together in their separateness. The only contact they have is through telling dirty jokes. Harry's appearance adds to Len's insecurity. Harry's Punch-and-Judy head poking round the door foreshadows his appearance and disappearance in Mary's seduction scene with Len later in the play. It says more about the relationships in the household than any dialogue could. Len gains time by simulating an orgy.

In **Scene Two,** we know that Len has moved in and that he and Pam share a bed regularly. There is a show of intimacy. For once, they have their own 'space' in the only place they could find it: on a boat in the middle of a lake. However, they don't know how to be intimate. They make plans for the future but without any coherent intent and Len keeps destroying their attempt at togetherness by asking questions. Pam has never reflected on anything in her life. She has not been taught to and it makes her extremely uncomfortable. Then Fred appears on the horizon. Pam is immediately attracted to his flashy confidence. This is the man who will protect her. Len is reduced to the role of observer with feeble attempts to join in the banter. He is slipping into the role, that of observer and helper, which will be his dominant one in the play.

In **Scene Three,** also set in the park, the young men are spending their lunch hour bantering and joking. The banter is a means of resisting their situation; they don't have access to other means. It is important that they are not teenagers. It would be too easy to pigeonhole them. Barry, the youngest, is twenty. Again, it is interesting that Fred is not with them. Fred is often, somehow, apart from the others, while being something of a dominant figure. The group show a great deal of nervous energy. They have nothing to do with their energy but self-destruct. Their dead-end jobs only alienate them all the more as members of a society. The casual way they talk about the death of a child, the way Pete tries to build his role in the accident, show their need to demonstrate to each other that they are men and unfeeling. They are reinforcing the stereotype of a male that they have inherited. Barry, the youngest in the group and described in the cast list as 'fat', is generally picked on and made a butt of their jokes. He tries to build up his status by claiming that he has killed people while on National Service in the army. It is no accident that he is the one who instigates the 'fun' later, which leads to the murder of the baby, and the last one to throw a stone and spit on the baby. Interestingly, Pete, the oldest of the group at twenty-five, draws on a pipe while he talks casually about the coroner. This stops us from just seeing him as a young hooligan. The Oedipal dimension of the play begins when the young men start to make crude comments about Len and Mary, when all he is doing is waiting to give her a helping hand with the shopping.

In **Scene Four**, the continual struggle for dominance and control is played out between Mary and Harry over the light switch. The baby has been born and Pam and Len are already settling into the Mary-and-Harry pattern, bickering with each other, despite all their plans and mutual reassurances in Scene Two. In fact they all pick on someone else in the scene. Only Harry doesn't, he tries his best to stay out of it, 'I ain' gettin' involved. Bound to be wrong.' Fred is now Pam's reluctant boyfriend and the claimed father of her baby. We sense he is only there for what he can get out of it. Fred to Pam, 'Got plenty of fags?' The TV dominates the scene. It needs fixing but they cannot afford to have it mended or buy a new one. Mary adjusts it some seven times. It drip-feeds a dead culture into the room. The baby cries from early in the scene. 'It' is ignored, even by Len. 'It'll cry itself to sleep,' he says. At times 'it' 'screams with rage'. Len eats his food steadfastly throughout the scene. Again, it shows he is not some species outside the others but born into the same culture with many of the shared limitations. The food has been carefully prepared for him by Mary. He is important now, as a source of income. We never see her prepare food for Harry or Pam although we presume she does cook for her daughter. It is one of the most horrific scenes in the play. The baby only sobs itself to sleep when Harry is left alone in the dark so he can have a sleep. The audience is denied any resolution to the scene.

Scene Five was a late addition to the play: 'the scene where the baby is on the bed was added after the play was written, and is really unnecessary – nothing happens that isn't made plain somewhere else. But somehow I felt that before the killing it was necessary to sum things up for the audience' (Bond in Hay and Roberts, 1980:

47). Pam has had the flu but has made herself ill over Fred's non-interest in her. Pam's nervous instability becomes more apparent. Len is extraordinarily attentive to Pam, giving her her medicine, straightening the bed, asking her if she's read her magazines. He's even bought tickets for him and Fred to go to the football match so Fred will come round. He works against his own interests. Len brings in the baby and for the first time, near the end of Scene Five, we learn from Len that it is a boy,

LEN (*looks at child*). 'E's well away.

It is the only time so far in the play that the child has not been referred to as 'it'. Pam utterly rejects the child and doesn't even want it on the bed with her.

Scene Six is the longest in the play and is a good example of the careful crafting that goes into all the scenes and, in fact, into all of Bond's plays. As it has become such a notorious scene, it will pay to look at it in some detail.

The scene starts with a curiously peaceful interlude before the brutality that comes later, despite the fact that Len constantly disturbs the peace by his need to ask questions. Fishing is traditionally one of the key areas where working-class people can 'de-alienate' themselves for a short while. I'm not suggesting that no other section of society fishes but just referring to the peculiar attraction that sitting on a tranquil river bank, apparently doing nothing, seems to have for so many working-class people. During their working lives, all the people in the play, like most of the rest of us, are alienated. In a Marxist sense, this means that they are disconnected from the reality of what they are doing. They are functioning to the requirements of the machine in a factory, for example: in a key sense, the machine operates them. When fishing, they are in charge and control of what they do. They see the direct results of their actions in the world. They are not agents in an unseen, unknown, chain of commodity production in capitalist society. In this scene they are, presumably, by the lake in the park although it could be a river flowing through the park, which would be even more powerful an image. For perhaps the only time in the play, there is a real attempt at human communication. It is almost as though Fred is an older brother with Len as his younger sidekick. Fred is asserting his greater economic know-how, 'You get 'em on h.p.', in reply to Len's 'Can't afford it', and his sexual

superiority, 'More like that! (*He holds his hands three feet apart.*)'.
He demonstrates his superior skill at fishing in an extraordinary
explanation of how to bait the hook with a worm. It is probably
the most words strung together by one character anywhere in the
play. It is extremely sensate. It is an immediate connection with the
real world not mediated through alienation or ideology. It is a piece
of teaching, 'Come 'ere. Look' (Fred), given without any sarcasm or
unkindness. Then when he casts the line, '*The line hums*' and Fred
simply says, 'Lovely'. It is another sensate moment, when he is
making contact with what is happening: his hand will feel the line
run out as well as hearing it. It is the opposite to the violence that
comes later and, in fact, the antithesis, the quiet heart, of all the
disconnection and bickering and jibing that permeates the play. He
even feeds the worms on milk. This is not to say that Fred is
presented as in any way perfect. He puts Len down, 'Oi – Len, I
come out for the fishin'. I don't wanna 'ear all your ol'crap.' But it
is banter, not cruel. Fred is insensitive and Len's greater sensitivity
is apparent, 'Well yer got a let 'er know' (that Fred is not coming
round). Len shares the intimate detail that he heard him in bed with
Pam. Then there is the one exchange where the communication
becomes real and between equals.

> LEN. On my life. Kep me up 'alf the night. Yer must a bin trying for the
> cup.
> FRED (*draws on his cigarette*). Why didn't yer let on?
> LEN. No, it's all a giggle, ain't it?
> FRED (*shrugs*). Yeh? Makes yer feel a right Charlie.
>
> *He drops his cigarette on the ground and treads on it.*
>
> Chriss. Thass one good reason for jackin' 'er in.
> LEN. Don't start blamin' me.
> FRED. An' you was listenin'?
> LEN. Couldn't 'elp it.
> FRED. O.
>
> *He lays his rod on the ground and crouches to pack his things.*
>
> Yer didn't mind me goin' round 'er's.
> LEN. Same if I did.
> FRED. I didn't know like.
> LEN. Yer never ruddy thought. Any'ow, I don't mind.

It both illustrates Len's loneliness and the anguish he must have felt
but there is also some dignity for Len here.

Mike comes in, who, likewise, has been fishing. He and Fred plan to go 'out on the 'unt', later that night. It is significant that they are going hunting for women. Some of the young men come on later, dressed in their best clothes to go 'hunting'. Pam comes on with the baby in the pram, the baby dosed up with aspirins.[1] From here on the scene moves away rapidly from its tranquil opening. Pam pleads for Fred to come round, abasing herself to a point where she says she doesn't mind if he goes with other girls. She obviously knows he is already seeing Liz. Fred denies it is his child and finally finishes with her. He tells her to 'piss off' and Pam retorts with 'An' yer can take yer bloody bastard round yer tart's! Tell 'er it's a present from me!' It is a real low point of abuse and neglect of the unwanted child. She leaves the pram behind.

The other young men come in and the whole devastating last section of the scene begins. It builds step by step. It is a logical sequence. They start 'harmlessly' playing about: comparing the baby's face to Fred's, making jokes, using the balloon as a phallic symbol. It is predictably Barry who starts it all. From the point that Colin pretends to be shot, when the balloon bursts, and Barry runs over him with the pram, the 'game' changes and the language changes. Pete 'touches' Barry and then the swearing starts and the 'game' with the pram starts to get violent and serious. The pushing of the pram at each other acts as a catalyst for their nervous energy to take a more sinister form. They start projecting all their frustrations on to the baby in the pram. However, again, it does not develop in an even line. There are some mild shows of concern for the baby. Colin: 'Go easy. […] Do leave off.' Later, it is Pete who says, ''E'll 'ave the little perisher out!' This is picked up by Barry who reminds him he had boasted of running down a child, which brings a violent pushing of the pram from Pete to Barry. While this is going on Fred and Mike are sitting separately and planning how they are going to get some women that night. It is important that they are not involved to start with. As the violence towards the baby builds, so the language changes.

---

[1] In the first version of Scene Six the pram was to be abandoned on its own in the park. Then a single stranger would turn up and set fire to it. But this would show only that isolated acts of madness are possible. It would still be theatre. Bond wanted the analysis to penetrate deeper into the community to find the causes there. Theatre stops at explanations, drama seeks explanations for explanations. This is the intention behind all his work.

PETE. Little bleeder.

He jerks the pram violently.

That knocked the grin off its face.

Fred sits sullenly downstage all this time with his back to the others. Many directors want to involve him in the business with the pram too soon – they say that would be his inevitable reaction. Bond says it is only the conventional reaction. The reality is he is brooding on the row with Pam, immersed in the problems of his own life. This is an instance of the need to 'play the play', not the conventionalised character. So Bond makes Fred wait till extraordinarily late before he intervenes in the scene. This creates an image of the truth of the whole society. He wants nothing to do with the baby but the others draw him in.

The scene is built up step by step. At each new step there is the chance for the violence to stop. The actors must know why they don't stop it. An instance of this is the jacket. Bond says if the jacket had not been spoilt the baby would not have been killed. So what 'meaning' does the jacket have for Colin? What did it cost? How important is it to his social image? Why does Barry say it came off a 'barrer'? What value cathects it? In flawed productions the carefully staged escalation is reduced to tensions *within* the 'gang'. But the text constantly relates to tensions *outside* the 'gang'. Society is not violent because there are gangs, there are gangs because society is violent. All the devices and techniques of Bond's theatre are deployed to put this 'reality' on the stage. It is the purpose of his drama. If this is ignored, this scene, one of the most famous in modern drama, is reduced to the emptiness of Hollywood nihilism. When Fred is goaded into throwing the first stone, he misses, probably on purpose. Then an incredible fury is unleashed. What is the meaning of this fury? The language is now extreme.

PETE. Get its 'ooter.
BARRY. An its slasher.

This is now the language that a lynch mob would use against the young men. It is strangely like the self-righteous screaming of the housewives in the next scene might have been. In their hurry to leave and save their own skins the violence even spreads to a fight between Pete and Barry, the latter so obsessed with the violence that he is holding up the escape.

PETE. Leave it!

BARRY. Juss this one!

He throws a stone as PETE *pushes him over. It goes wide.*

Bastard!

To PETE. Yer put me off!

PETE. I'll throttle yer!

Bond describes an acting exercise he has used with the actors at this point. He gets them all to shout at the pram as loudly as possible and then asks them who they are shouting at. They answer, 'The baby.' He repeats this as often as six or seven times and each time the shouting gets more ferocious and they give the same answer but eventually when he asks who they are shouting at, they reply, 'Ourselves.' The exercise has always had the same result.

> In *Saved* I think a proper understanding of the stoning scene is that the gang are in an important sense stoning themselves – important in a cultural and political sense. (Bond, 2001: 182)

They subconsciously see themselves in the dirty, excrement-smeared, helpless object in the pram. The audience is not to be allowed to see the stoning as, for example, an exercise in sadism. This would avoid the audience being able to see the social/cultural implication of the act. The way it is acted becomes crucial. This involves the actors being aware of the site they are occupying at this moment. It is not just a question of the individual psychology of each character but of the sum total of society's influences on them at this time: their economic/social situation.

> The audience judges in the same complex way that it judges in ordinary life. But it is given this advantage: it may look at things it would normally run from in fear, turn from in embarrassment, prevent in anger, or pass by because they are hidden, either purposefully or innocently. So the audiences respond with all the faculties of their consciousness to the things that determine their social and private lives. (Bond cited in Hirst, 1985: 24)

It is the actors' responsibility to enable this to happen. In an exercise he first used with actors at the Theatre Studio in Alfortville, Paris, Bond describes how the actor has to approach the characters.

> For instance, its important that – in the stoning – the young man's jacket is, early on, made dirty – and that then he later on shows disgust at the baby's dirtiness – because he sees in the baby an image of himself trying

to overcome the triviality – the dirt – of his own existence. So for that young man there is a specific edge to his disgust at the baby. It isn't generalised as character – it probes further: its as if the young man sees the whole of existence as a Manichean[1] struggle between dirt and cleanliness – and so why in this scene does he actively take the part of dirt (destruction)? – as if in the scene he is attacking not himself (which he is) but the baby. Now this opens up enormous possibilities for the actor. Its as if – in the moment when he shows disgust – he has to combine self-pity, self-rage, the delicacy of cleanliness (though that may become a puritan horror) with the savagery of poverty – almost anything but not just plain 'anger'. (Bond, 2008e) [Punctuation as in original]

This involves the actor finding the way of exposing the Invisible Object, the complex layers of meaning expressed in this above. The need for justice becomes the desire for other victims/revenge.

If enacted to bring out the Invisible Object, the stoning scene produces moments of Accident Time, the audience are confronted with the sort of society we are creating. They are on their own Site: the Site of imagination. There is no escape. We have to search for our humanity or deny it. There is no Brechtian alienation here. There is the aim to connect with the audience's Radical Innocence: the human imperative to seek justice in the world but through direct confrontation, in the event as it were, not sitting outside just judging others. Objects are used to build the scene's meanings. Some of these are used unconventionally: a nappy is swung round above the head as if it were a football rattle. The audience are confronted with the Gap. The opaque window pane of ideology is smashed and the objective reality of the event is shown in Accident Time: the sort of society we are all creating. This complex process can only succeed if the play is *en*acted to open out the Invisible Object.

Then there is the 'curious buzzing'. Bond has described this buzzing as trying to create a charged atmosphere, like change in air pressure after a big event such as an earthquake (Bond, 2008a). Bond's plays are not limited to only one interpretation. They are open and indeed require creative realisation but only in terms of how the play is written.

When Pam comes back to collect the baby, she seems in a hazed state. We know she has been taking tablets like her mum. She coos to the child, who she doesn't even notice is dead, smeared with

---

[1] Seeing everything in stark terms of good/evil, cleanliness/dirtiness.

excrement, smelly, filthy and bruised: the sing-song to the child is as though she is comforting herself. She is so self-centred, necessarily so, because she has not been made to feel at home in the world but rather she has disappeared into herself and cannot even use her immediate sensate experience to connect with the world. Again, the audience is denied any resolution to this scene.

This is only a preliminary, and individual, examination of the scene. It is an example of how finely textured Bond's dialogue is and how deceptively simple it appears to be. We can begin to see how his drama works, and the direction in which it will develop throughout his later plays has already been set.

In **Scene Seven** there is, again, the usual jump in the plot line, marked by the clanging of a steel door. Fred has been arrested and is in a police cell awaiting his court appearance. He comes in with a mack over his head that is covered in spit. This is another unconventional use of an object. It is not covered with spots of rain but with spit. As Bond develops the use of objects in later plays we can imagine an object such as this mack appearing more than once and being cathexed and decathexed with different values and meanings. Fred's indignation against the women who have covered him in spit is interesting. In a sense, they are behaving as the young men have done. They are probably the mothers of Mike, Barry, Pete and so on; they are just as much victims of society's inability to be human. They also need to vent their anger at their own situation against a visible enemy: they are a lynch mob. Len, as usual, has thought of Fred's needs, brings him cigarettes and gives him advice as to how to manage the cigarettes inside. He tells him to expect a remand in custody. Fred seems to be in denial about what has happened, blaming Pam for leaving the baby, blaming the others. Almost like a little boy he rehearses what he might say in court while wanting to deny to Pam that he was involved, 'Lot a roughs. Never seen 'em before. Don't arst me. Blokes like that anywhere. I tried to chase them off.' Pam is her usual needy self, going through the motions of what she has picked up from the TV or the radio about what a woman should do in this sort of situation. The song 'Stand by Your Man', although not released until 1968, describes perfectly what the phoney pop culture around her tells her she should do. 'Sometimes it's hard to be a woman … sometimes it's hard to give your love to just one man … even though he's hard to understand … give him your arms to cling to', and so on. Fred at one stage '*puts his arms around her waist and leans his head against her*'. She tries to find the lines that have not been written for her, not quite rising to the 'cultural' norms of the song. 'I'll buy a pad on me way 'ome.' It's a bathetic attempt to give love but she does write to him while he's in prison. She is doing her best.

It is important that Len appears and we know he was a witness. He did not appear in earlier drafts of the play but it is important to establish that he is as responsible, morally, as the others. If he had not witnessed the murder, he would not have been able to learn from it. He is, later, able to see through Fred, who has been something of a role model for him earlier in the play.

In **Scene Eight** Fred is about to be released from prison. Again, we learn of this through a one-liner, 'Yer mate's comin' out'. Len and Harry exchange a few sociable words. Len is the only person Harry bothers to try to communicate with. He is doing his own ironing. It seems as though he only has one shirt and this one is nearly worn out. Pam spends the whole scene drying her hair. Bond suggested to the actor playing Pam in one production that she should cover her head the whole time, even speaking through the towel, not poking her head out until the end of the scene (Bond, 2008e). This, again, is working for the Invisible Object: Pam has almost disappeared as a person; Fred has been in prison; her unwanted baby is dead. Her continual worrying about Fred is interesting, she wants to give him a 'home' in her house and has her eyes on Len's room. She never shows that she loves Fred or that she even knows anything about giving love. In fact, she appears as a person with no ability to feel for other people. She continually feels only her own emptiness. She needs Fred, like she first needed Len, to fill that emptiness in herself. She is anxious about Fred's imminent release and whether or not he'll want her. The means of attacking Len becomes the search for or rather the raging about the lost *Radio Times*. The overt fury of the stoning becomes the repressed fury in the house.

Scene Nine in some ways parallels the opening scene where Pam seduces Len and Harry pops in and straight out. Len is in the room first, so when Mary comes in wearing her slip, it is a deliberate provocation. She has earlier told Pam off for wandering about in her slip. Mary has probably had a series of affairs when she was younger and Harry has intimated as much. Here she is almost wanting to relive some of what has disappeared from her life. She knows very well what she is doing throughout the scene. 'Bite it', referring to the thread, is as close an invitation as she is able to make and she knows what it will do to Harry who has just come in for his football pools. Len is much more daring with his remarks than we might imagine. The Oedipal dimension is not completed however, probably because Harry has come in or because that was as far as Mary wanted to take it. In fact Mary is probably aiming to manipulate Harry as well as Len or she would have approached Len when Harry was at work not when she herself was about to go out. Len masturbates instead.

Scene Ten is set in a café and Len and Pam are waiting to greet Fred on his release. We have to guess at the time lapse but if Fred received a sentence for manslaughter we must be talking about two or three years minimum. However, this is immaterial to the development of the play. Some time has passed and that is all that is relevant. When Fred arrives we see that the young men have changed. Their language is different. They are there grudgingly, condemned by their own repressed guilt. There is no real camaraderie. The crude jokes are still there but there is a palpable edge.

> PETE (*to* FRED). What yer fancy?
> FRED. What they got? [...] Juss bring the lot.
> PETE. Oi, ease off.
> FRED. An' four cups a tea.
> PETE. I'm standin' yer for this!

Later in the scene Fred offers to pay for his food.

> PETE. 'Oo arst yer t' pay?
> FRED. I reckon it's worth one lousy meal.
> PETE. Yer made yer own decision, didn't yer?
> BARRY (*comes down*). Wass up?
> PETE: We ain' got a crawl up yer arse.

Pam tries to remake contact with Fred but he is clearly with Liz permanently now and is harsh towards her: 'Yer should a read them crummy letters she keeps sendin'. She ain' goin' a catch me round 'er place.'

Liz asks a 'surface' question – what was it like inside prison – and Fred repeats 'cold' and then there is a silence. This silence is the coldness of society, the silence of the cold, dead baby. This isn't a Pinter silence because its meaning is acidly clear. The actors need to experience the cold silence. Extraordinarily, Len wants to know from Fred what it was like to kill the baby. Or, rather, it is not extraordinary. Len's need to know about death is the sign that of all of them he is aware of mortality, without which we cannot be human. Len's question provokes a violent response – for the gang, looking at reality always produces a violent response. The juke-box and the demand for 'My 'Eart is Broken' is more of the pop culture that shapes their perception of the world.

Scene Eleven brings the repressed violence and hatred in the house to a head and out into the open. It echoes the violence in the park. The battle starts in the same way that it has always been, silently, over control of space and material objects until, finally, it comes into the open as Mary tips Harry's tea on to the floor, followed by his bread. Then Mary moves from silent action to words and pours out her frustration with her life situation. They are talking at last but only with as much mutual recrimination as possible. Harry moves towards her giving some intention of retaliating physically and trips over the chair and the leg breaks off. The violence crescendos with Mary cracking the teapot over Harry's head as we have explored above. Len tries to stop the row between them probably because he intuits the cause, the stocking incident – in fact he then tries to stop Harry telling Pam about it. He knows it will throw fuel on the fire. When Pam learns what has happened between Mary and Len she goes into hysterics. There is the fight over the knife. Pam continually expresses the final despair and sense of doom she has about life and her final sense of abandonment: 'No 'ome. No friends. Baby dead. Gone. Fred gone.' Len offers to leave. Ironically, Pam doesn't hear it because she is too busy asking for it.

Scene Twelve is the most sinister scene in the play. It has the formal sense of Harry coming in to be friendly and to encourage Len to stay. Len is still engrossed with Pam and thinks she might have a man downstairs. However, Harry is dressed like a ghost. He is non-existent and he has come to try to get Len to stay and join him, eventually to become like him. In fact, he is like an emissary coming on behalf of the family. They all sense that they need him for their different reasons but none of those reasons is in Len's best interests. Harry, here, is a totally corrupting, corrosive influence. Len takes the opportunity to find out about what it was like in the war and there is an unusual response from Harry. 'Yer never killed yer man.

Yer missed that. Gives yer a sense a perspective. I was one a the
lucky ones.' It is an overt statement. I think the only time this occurs
in the play. It echoes Barry's 'Shootin' up the yeller-niggers'. Len is
making a half-hearted attempt to pack but by the end of the scene,
he does not want to stay. By the next scene he has, however, decided
to stay. He can't just cast these people aside in their misery. He has
come down from his tree, where he was an observer of the stoning,
to mend the chair.

Scene Thirteen we have already examined. It is worth noting the
way it is constructed. Mary, Pam and Harry are not carrying on in
their usual way. It is an extreme. They are the living dead, while,
apart from them, Len is trying to repair the chair that was broken in
the quarrel. He has made a very clear decision to stay between the
last scene and this one. From the uncertainty of the bangs off stage
(pistol shots or a hammer?) we move to the absolute certainty of a
chair in a man's hands. He is trying to move the family forward. We
feel he may not succeed in this but he will not give up trying.

Design
In Bond's plays, the design is integral to the structure. If the design
isn't right then nothing will work, as Chris Cooper of Big Brum has
remarked. He means you have to get the set structurally right
because it operates like a site. The Greek and Jacobean stages had
the social site built into their site, the fabric of the theatre. Now we
have only an empty space or one adorned with a pretty frame.
    The first production of *Saved* is described in Hay and Roberts's
book (1980: 57). Bill Gaskill, the director, describes how Bond told
him the triangle-shaped room 'was like a bowling-alley. I'd never
seen a piece of scenery like that before. It has a kind of enclosing
feeling. I don't think I've ever seen it used before or since. A real,
imaginative invention. And then in front of that, we just had the
necessary furniture.' Eight of the play's thirteen scenes were played
on this set. The park scenes were done on the 'bare stage, the café
scene just had chairs and table without the flats, and the cell scene
was a simple door-flat' (ibid.). This confined space of the 'living-
room' allows the preoccupation with space to be brought out. *My
Radio Times*, *my* teapot, *my* cup, and so on. It is also like a tomb or
coffin for the living dead. The precise sparseness of the scenery
allows the focus to be on the objects. A few simple objects in each

scene provide the means of exploring the meaning of the situation. Design, for Bond, is the immediate Site of the play and carries this importance in it. It needs to be integral to the play's text and centre.

Language
Earlier I quoted Bond as saying that we have no language for the reality of our lives. Like so many of Bond's apparently straightforward sayings, it contains massive philosophical, sociological and political implications. I understand him to mean that the Greeks and Shakespeare's England had a language that worked for everything from the highest thoughts to the most menial tasks. The Greeks had their mythology, which provided a common understanding of themselves and the world around them. In Shakespeare's time, there was the great Chain of Being, which ordered everything in their known universe, from God to humans to rocks and trees. Bond has taken as an example of this use of language for the highest thoughts down to the day-to-day, Hesiod's *Theogony* and *Works and Days*. Hesiod was one of the earliest Greek poets and lived about 700 BC. The first of these works was one of the original formalisations of Greek mythology – it deals with the creation of the universe and the origin of morality, the justice of Zeus. Bond sees this as an unconscious reconstruction of the world of the neonate. The second, *Works and Days*, describes the opposite, the social, objective world of the later adult self. It gives day-to-day details to farmers about how and when to plant their crops and so on. It is extraordinary that the same language worked for both seemingly opposite purposes. It meant that language was able to nurture and chasten human consciousness into the creative relationship with its historical world that produced the brilliance of Greek civilisation and its drama. Both still influence us profoundly. Bond argues that we have no language that will do for both. This leads him to use demotic language in many of his plays: the language of day-to-day communication, of the people. This is the language of his latest groups of plays, the Colline pentad and the Big Brum plays:

> I try to put into demotic street language the insights and profundities that Shakespeare and other tragic and comic dramatists put into the mouths of princes and the highly educated. This is because reality has lost its language. Shakespeare's characters' language belonged to the church, the pub, the street, the council chamber. None of these places was silent or

obscure to the others, when they disagreed they agreed on what the disagreement was about. By comparison we are in a highly structured chaos. Since the enlightenment we are fractured into specialised languages of science, bureaucracy, the media, consumerism and so on. We cannot speak of, from or to our *selves*. Hamlet could talk to himself (in his soliloquies) and to the gravediggers. We are silent to our *self* – which means that we cannot create our *self*. In my plays I seek to put people (the characters and the audience) in extreme situations where they must speak to themselves and thus, each of them, create a *self*. (Bond, 2008f)

Saved is an early example of this approach to language.

Conclusion

I have tried in this introduction to give some sense of the scope of Bond's dramaturgy, his politics and philosophy, and a guide to how his plays need to be approached. This leads to a final word about the extraordinary range of the rest of Bond's work, which needs to become so much better known.

All Bond's plays ask 'What is it to be human?' He reverses the Brechtian formula in which the general interprets and explains the particular, and instead uses the particular to *prove and justify* the general.

His drama deals with the individual struggling for self-understanding in a society where people live in widely different circumstances. The plays make it clear that this struggle can succeed only by making society more just – the two things are indivisible. The formula might be: 'My humanness, your justice'. His other main concern is in a profound way a consequence of this first struggle: it is the form of drama itself. He believes that the creation of drama came out of this struggle – it's what drama *is*. So he has searched for a modern drama which enables each of us to understand our self and our society, in the way Greek and Jacobean drama had made this possible in their own societies. But he sees a fundamental difference in that in Greek drama the characters and audiences had a mythic-sacred cover, and in Jacobean drama a religious-political cover, but modern humans are 'raw and uncovered and must create a social(ist) self in a world of frantic media and conflicting information' (Bond, 2008g).

His plays fall into six series. The first series from *Pope's Wedding* to *The Sea*, formed a survey, 'both respecting and critical', of existing drama (Bond, 2008g). The second series, from *Bingo* to *Human Cannon*, took a close look at particular problems uncovered in the first series, such as the political role of received literature (*Bingo*), the idealisation of the classics (*The Woman*) and social-war politics (*Human Cannon*). The third series, *The War Plays*, uses the understanding developed in the earlier series to explore societies in extreme situations. These plays are set in and after an atomic war – but the symptoms and political consequences of that war would also be those of our present looming ecological catastrophe, if we do not prevent it in time. The fourth series includes *Jackets*, *The Company of Men*, *Olly's Prison*, *Tuesday* and *Derek*, and works to create a new political drama after the collapse of Stalinism. Bond believes that this collapse was already implicit in the first three series. The fifth series consists of two interrelated cycles. One is the Big Brum plays: *At the Inland Sea*, *Eleven Vests*, *Have I None*, *The Balancing Act*, *The Under Room* and *Tune*, and two other short plays, *Chair* and *Existence*. The other cycle is the Colline pentad, *Coffee*, *The Crime of the Twenty-First Century*, *Born*, *People* and *Innocence*. The pentad moves from the present into the future. Bond regards the plays in these two cycles as the most radical he has so far written. The sixth series will deal with the developing crisis, which is now not just a social crisis but a species crisis. He believes we are reaching the limit which evolution can tolerate, and if we pass this limit we will enter into a regressive de-civilisation. This makes the later plays even more urgent. Bond says, 'they are written in the silence of *Saved*' (Bond, 2008a).

He has long warned us of the shortage of time:

> We have to understand the dangers, the opportunities and the shortage of time. Time is no longer a benign old man with a white beard, a staff and a lantern. It is a crying child tugging at our sleeve and asking to be carried. (Bond, 1974)

To adapt a quote from Bond: in constructing a human future now we are like 'architects [trying] to design houses in a leaking boat in the middle of an ocean' (Bond, 1996a). Clearly, we need more Lens.

References

Bellow, S. (2007/1987) *More Die of Heartbreak*, Harmondsworth: Penguin Modern Classics

Belsay, C. (2002) *Poststructuralism: A Very Short Introduction*, Oxford: OUP

Benedetti, J. (1982) *Stanislavski: An Introduction*, London: Methuen

Benedetti, J. (1991) *The Moscow Art Theatre Letters*, London: Methuen Drama

Billington, M. (2008) *Guardian*, 24 January 2008

Bond, E. (1974) 'A Note on the Play' in Wedekind, F., *Spring Awakening*, transl. Edward Bond, London: Methuen Drama

Bond, E. (1995) 'Notes on Imagination' in *Coffee*, London: Methuen Drama

Bond, E. (1996a) 'Playing About', a talk to students at the Centre for Studies in Drama in Education, University of Central England (unpublished)

Bond, E. (1996b) *Edward Bond: Letters III*, UK: Harwood Academic Publishers

Bond, E. (1998a) 'Commentary on the War Plays' in *Edward Bond: Plays 6*, London: Methuen Drama

Bond, E. (1998b) workshop with Edward Bond working on TEs, Brecht and Stanislavski for the Centre for Studies in Drama in Education at the University of Central England of which Bond was the patron for some ten years

Bond, E. (2000) *The Hidden Plot: Notes on Theatre and the State*, London: Methuen

Bond, E. (2001) *Edward Bond: Letters 5* (ed. I. Stuart), London: Routledge

Bond, E. (2002) extract from 'The Fourth Story: A Short Treatise on Self, Society and Modern Acting', unpublished paper

Bond, E. (2003) *Edward Bond: Plays 7*, London: Methuen Drama

Bond, E. (2004) seminar in Newman College, Birmingham, with contributors to D. Davis (ed.), *Edward Bond and the Dramatic Child*, Stoke-on-Trent: Trentham Books

Bond, E. (2006) 'The Translucency of Drama', unpublished paper

Bond, E. (2007) 'Some Notes on *The Sea*', unpublished

Bond, E. (2008a) interview between Bond and the author

Bond, E. (2008b) unpublished extract from notebooks

Bond, E. (2008c) unpublished letter to the author

Bond, E. (2008d) unpublished letter to the author

Bond, E. (2008e) unpublished letter to Emmanuel Matte

Bond, E. (2008f) unpublished letter to Laszlo Upor

Bond, E. (2008g) unpublished letter to the author

Brecht, B. (1978/1964) *Brecht on Theatre: The Development of an Aesthetic*, ed. J. Willett, London: Eyre Methuen

Chomsky, N. (2004) *Hegemony or Survival: America's Quest for Global Dominance*, Harmondsworth: Penguin Books

Cooper, C. (2005) 'Edward Bond and the Big Brum Plays', in D. Davis (ed.), *Edward Bond and the Dramatic Child*, Stoke-on-Trent: Trentham Books

De Jongh, N. (2001) *Politics, Prudery and Perversion: the Censoring of the English Stage 1901–1968*, London: Methuen

Dostoevsky, F. (2004) *The Brothers Karamazov*, London: Vintage Books

Eddershaw, M. (1996) *Performing Brecht*, London: Routledge

Fuegi, J. (1987) *Bertolt Brecht: Chaos, According to Plan*, Cambridge: CUP

Hay, M. and Roberts, P. (1980) *Bond: A Study of his Plays*, London: Eyre Methuen

Hirst, D. L. (1985) *Edward Bond*, London: Macmillan

Katafiasz, K. (2005) 'Alienation is the Theatre of Auschwitz', in D. Davis (ed.), *Edward Bond and the Dramatic Child*, Stoke-on-Trent: Trentham Books

Mogose, R. (2007) *Is Brecht's epic theatre still relevant in recent theatre?*, BA thesis, University of Portsmouth http://dissertations.port.ac.uk/212/01/MogoseR.pdf

Olivier, L. (1965) cited by Bond in a letter to the *Daily Telegraph*, 6 December 1965 in the Bond Archive, Victoria and Albert Theatre Museum

Scharine, R. (1976) *The Plays of Edward Bond*, London: Associated University Press

Stiglitz, J. (2002) *Globalization and Its Discontents*, Harmondsworth: Penguin Books

Toporkov, V. O. (1979) *Stanislavski in Rehearsal: The Final Years*, London: Routledge

Willett, J. (1964) *The Theatre of Bertolt Brecht* (2nd ed.), London: Methuen

Willett, J. (1967) *The Theatre of Bertolt Brecht* (3rd ed.), London: Methuen

Willett, J. (1998) *Brecht in Context* (revised ed.), London: Methuen

Further Reading

Belsay, C. (2002) *Poststructuralism: A Very Short Introduction*,
Oxford: OUP
(An extremely useful and accessible introduction to
poststructuralism.)
Bond, E. (1995) 'Notes on Imagination' in *Coffee*, London:
Methuen Drama
(Essential reading to come to grips with the key importance of
imagination in Bond's work.)
Bond, E. (2000) *The Hidden Plot: Notes on Theatre and the State*,
London: Methuen
(The most important resource to understand Bond's theoretical
thinking which underpins all his work.)
Bond, E. (2000) *Selections from the Notebooks of Edward Bond*,
Vol. One: 1959 to 1980, ed. and intro. Ian Stuart, London:
Methuen
Bond, E. (2001) *Selections from the Notebooks of Edward Bond*,
Vol. Two: 1980 to 1995, ed. and intro. Ian Stuart, London:
Methuen
(Both these *Notebooks* provide extremely interesting insights
into the artist at work.)
Bond, E. (2001) *Edward Bond – Letters 5*, ed. Ian Stuart, London:
Routledge
(Another invaluable resource where Bond comments on his plays
and his ideas on drama, society and culture.)
Bond, E. (2006) 'Freedom and Drama' in *Edward Bond: Plays 8*,
London: Methuen Drama
(Again, essential reading: a concise account of key dimensions of
Bond's work.)
Davis, D. (ed.) (2005) *Edward Bond and the Dramatic Child*,
Stoke-on-Trent: Trentham Books
(The only book in English to give a recent and full account of
Bond's approach to his new form of drama with case studies of
his plays for young people, including a full glossary of terms.)

Hawkes, D. (1996) *Ideology*, London: Routledge
   (A usefully wide-ranging small book about the history of
   ideology: almost a small manual on philosophy. Quite difficult,
   but rewarding, for beginners.)

SAVED

Author's Note

Saved is almost irresponsibly optimistic. Len, the chief character, is good in spite of his upbringing and environment, but he is not wholly or easily good because then his goodness would be meaningless, at least for himself.

It is true that at the end of the play Len does not know what he will do next, but then he never has done. The play ends in silent social stalemate, but if audiences think this is pessimistic that is because they have not learned to clutch at straws. Clutching at straws is the only realistic thing to do. The alternative, apart from the self-indulgence of pessimism, is a fatuous optimism. The gesture of turning the other cheek is often a way of refusing to look facts in the face. This is not true of Len. He lives with people at their most hopeless (that is the point of the final scene) and does not turn away from them. I cannot imagine an optimism more tenacious or honest than this.

By not playing his traditional role in the play's tragic Oedipal pattern, Len turns it into what is formally a comedy. The Oedipal outcome should be a quarrel and death. There is a quarrel and even a struggle with a knife – but Len continues to try to understand and help. The next scene starts with him stretched on the floor with a knife in his hand and the old man comes in dressed as a ghost. But neither of them is dead. The only sensible object in defeating an enemy is to make him your friend.

Clearly the stoning to death of a baby in a London park is a typical English understatement. Compared to the 'strategic' bombing of cities it is a negligible atrocity. Compared to the cultural and emotional deprivation of most children its consequences are insignificant.

Almost all morality taught to children is grounded in religion. This in itself bewilders them – religion has nothing to do with their parents' personal lives, or our economic, industrial and political life, and is contrary to the science and reason they are taught at other times. For them religion discredits the morality it is meant to sustain. The result is that they grow up morally illiterate and cannot understand, because they have not been taught, the nature of a moral consideration or the value of morals at all. This is not always noticed because we use words that still have moral connotations, but these are being lost. Morals cannot be slapped on as a social lubricant. They must share a common basis with social organisation and be consistent with accepted knowledge. That means teaching understanding not faith.

Like most people I am a pessimist by experience but an optimist by nature. I shall go on being true to my nature. It is often a mistake to learn from experience.

CHARACTERS

LEN, *twenty-one. Tall, slim, firm, bony. Big hands. High, sharp cheekbones. Pleasant pale complexion – not ashen. Blue eyes, thick fair hair a bit oily, brushed sideways from a parting. Prominent feet.*

FRED, *twenty-one. Blond, very curly hair. Medium height. Well-shaped, steady, powerful body. Light tenor voice.*

HARRY, *sixty-eight. Tall. Long thin arms. Long hands. Heavy, bony head with large eye-sockets and small eyes. Loose chin. Grey.*

PETE, *twenty-five. Tallish. Well-built, red-faced. Makes very few gestures. Soft hair that tends to stick up lightly.*

COLIN, *shortish. A bit thin. Loose (but not big) mouth. Shiny ears, curved featureless face. A few spots. Shouts to make himself heard. Eighteen.*

MIKE, *tall. Well-built. Strong, easy, emphatic movements. Pleasant. Dark hair. Twenty.*

BARRY, *twenty. A little below medium height. Fat.*

PAM, *twenty-three. Thin, sharp-busted. Heavy, nodal hips. Dark hair. Long narrow face. Pale eyes. Small mouth. Looks tall from a distance, but is shorter than she looks.*

MARY, *fifty-three. Shortish. Round heavy shoulders. Big buttocks. Bulky breasts, lifeless but still high. Big thighs and little ankles. Curled grey hair that looks as if it is in a hair-net. Homely.*

LIZ, *exactly as she sounds.*

SETTING

The area of the play is South London.

The stage is as bare as possible – sometimes completely bare.

There should be an interval after Scene Seven.

Saved was first presented by the English Stage Company at the Royal Court Theatre, London, on 3 November 1965 with the following cast:

LEN	John Castle
FRED	Tony Selby
HARRY	Richard Butler
PETE	Ronald Pickup
COLIN	Dennis Waterman
MIKE	John Bull
BARRY	William Stewart
PAM	Barbara Ferris
MARY	Gwen Nelson
LIZ	Alison Frazer

Directed by William Gaskill
Assistant to Director Jane Howell
Designed by John Gunter
Stage Manager Juliet Alliston
Assistant to Stage Manager Allison Rockley

SCENE ONE

*The living-room. The front and the two side walls make a triangle
that slopes to a door back centre.*

*Furniture: table down right, sofa left, TV set left front,
armchair up right centre, two chairs close to the table.*

Empty.

The door opens. LEN *comes in. He goes straight out again.*

PAM (*off*). In there.

LEN *comes in. He goes down to the sofa. He stares at it.*

All right?

Pause. PAM *comes in.*

LEN. This ain' the bedroom.

PAM. Bed ain' made.

LEN. Oo's bothered?

PAM. It's awful. 'Ere's nice.

LEN. Suit yourself. Yer don't mind if I take me shoes off?
(*He kicks them off.*) No one 'ome?

PAM. No.

LEN. Live on yer tod?

PAM. No.

LEN. O.

Pause. He sits back on the couch.

Yer all right? Come over 'ere.

PAM. In a minit.

LEN. Wass yer name?

PAM. Yer ain' arf nosey.

LEN. Somethin' up?

PAM. Can't I blow me nose?

She puts her hanky back in her bag and puts it on the table.
Better.

She sits on the couch.

LEN. Wass yer name?

PAM. Wass yourn?

LEN. Len.

PAM. Pam.

LEN. O. (*He feels the couch behind with his hand.*) This big
enough?

PAM. What yer want? Bligh!

LEN. Don't wan' a push yer off. Shove that cushion up.

PAM. 'Ang on.

LEN. 'Ow often yer done this?

PAM. Don't be nosey.

LEN. Take yer shoes off.

PAM. In a minit.

LEN. Can yer move yer – thass better.

PAM. Yer d'narf fidget.

LEN. I'm okay now.

PAM. Ow!

LEN. D'yer 'ave the light on?

PAM. Suit yerself.

LEN. I ain' fussy.

PAM. Ow!

LEN. Can yer shut them curtains?

PAM *goes left to the curtains.*

Yer got a fair ol'arse.

PAM. Like your mug.

LEN. Know somethin'? – I ain' touched a tart for weeks.

PAM. Don't know what yer missin'.

LEN. Don't I?

PAM *sits on the couch, on the edge.* LEN *pulls her closer and takes off her shoes.*

Lucky.
PAM. What?
LEN. Bumpin' in t'you.
PAM. Yeh.
LEN. Yer don't mind me?
PAM. No.
LEN. Sure?
PAM. Yer wan'a get on with it.
LEN. Give us a shout if I do somethin' yer don't reckon.
PAM. Bligh! Yer ain' better 'ave.
LEN. I could go for you. Know that?

Pause.

This is the life.
PAM. Ow!
LEN. Sh! Keep quiet now.
PAM. Oi!
LEN. Sh!
PAM. Yer told me t'shout!

The door opens. HARRY *comes in. He goes straight out again.*

LEN (*lifts his head*). 'Ere!
PAM. What?
LEN. Oo's that?
PAM. Ol' man.
LEN (*sits*). Whass 'e want?
PAM. That cushion's stickin' in me back.
LEN. I thought yer reckon yer was on yer tod?
PAM. 'E's late for work.
LEN. O. Why?
PAM. Why?

LEN. Yeh.

PAM. I don't know.

LEN. Reckon 'e saw?

PAM. Shouldn't be surprised.

LEN. Will 'e be long?

PAM. Don't arst me.

LEN. O. Well.

They lie down again. Slight pause. LEN *lifts his head.*

'Ear that?

PAM. No.

LEN. I 'eard somethin'.

He goes to the door. He listens. He goes back to the couch and sits on the end.

PAM. Well?

LEN. Better 'ang on.

PAM. Why?

LEN. Better 'ad.

PAM. Think yer'll last?

LEN. Not if yer lie around like that.

PAM. Like what?

LEN. Sit up.

PAM. I juss got right.

LEN. More'n I 'ave. Chriss. (*He feels in his pocket.*) You smoke?

PAM. In me bag.

LEN. Where's yer bag?

PAM *nods at the table. He goes to the bag and takes out a cigarette. He lights it. He starts putting the cigarettes back.*

Oh, sorry.

He holds the packet out to her.

PAM. No thanks.

LEN (*he puts the cigarettes away. He sits on the edge of the*

couch. Pause. He taps his foot three or four times). Wass
  'is caper?
PAM. Wan'a cup 'a tea?
LEN. After.
PAM. 'E won't be long.
LEN. 'Adn't better. 'Ave a puff?
PAM. No.
LEN. Do yer dress up.
PAM. Sorry.
LEN. Yer never know 'oo's poppin' in.

He goes to the door and opens it.

PAM. You off?
LEN. I could'a swore I 'eard 'eavy breathin'.
PAM. Thass you.
LEN. 'Oo else yer got knockin' about? Yer ain't stuffed yer
  grannie under the sofa?
PAM. She's dead.
LEN. 'Ard luck. – Wass 'is caper?

He sits on a chair.

  My blinkin' luck.

He stands and walks.

  'E'll be late, won't 'e! I 'ope they dock 'is bloody packet.

He listens by the door.

  Not a twitter.
PAM. 'E ain' bin out the back yet.
LEN. The ol' twit.

PAM *laughs.*

  Wass the joke?
PAM. You.

LEN (*amused*). Yeh. Me. Ha! 'E's a right ol' twit, ain' 'e!
  'Ere, can I stay the night?
PAM. Ain' yer got nowhere?
LEN. Yeh! – Well?
PAM. No.
LEN. Yer're the loser. – Sure's 'e's goin'? – Why can't I?
PAM. Bligh! I only juss met yer.
LEN. Suppose 'e's stoppin' 'ome? Got a cold or somethin'.
  I'd do me nut! – Yer'd enjoy it.
PAM. Big 'ead.
LEN. 'Ow many blokes yer 'ad this week?
PAM. We ain't finished Monday yet!
LEN. We'll take that into consideration.
PAM. Saucy bugger!

They laugh.

  'Ow many times yer 'ad it this week?

LEN. I told yer once! 'Ow many blokes yer 'ad all told?

They laugh.

PAM. What about you an' girls?

LEN. Can't count over sixty.

They laugh.

PAM. Sh!

LEN. 'E'll 'ear. – Oi, tell us!

PAM. 'Ow many times yer done it in one night?

They laugh.

LEN. Why did the woman with three tits shoot 'erself?
PAM. Eh?
LEN. She only 'ad two nipples.

They laugh.

PAM. I don't get it. (*She laughs.*) What did the midwife say to the nun?

LEN. Don' know.

She whispers in his ear. They laugh.

You're great! What about the woman with three tits 'oo 'ad quads?

PAM. Eh?
LEN. That'll teach 'er t'sleep with siamese twins!

They laugh. He whispers in her ear.

PAM. Yer ought a be locked up!
LEN. That's a feedin' problem!
PAM. Sh – thass the back door. 'E's bin out the lav.
LEN. Less give 'im a thrill.

He jumps noisily on the couch.

Cor – blimey!
PAM. You're terrible!

He takes some sweets from her bag.

They're my sweets.
LEN. Less 'ave a choose. (*Loudly.*) 'Ow's that for size?
PAM. What yer shoutin?
LEN (*he puts a sweet in her mouth*). Go easy! Yer wanna make it last!

She laughs. He bites a sweet in half and looks at it.

Oo, yer got a lovely little soft centre.
(*Aside to* PAM). First time I seen choclit round it!

He jumps on the sofa.

PAM (*shrill*). Yer awful!
LEN. That still 'ard?

PAM (*laughs*). Leave off!

LEN. Come on, there's plenty more where that come from.

He puts a sweet in her mouth.

PAM (*splutters*). Can't take no more!

LEN. Yeh – open it. Yer can do a bit more!

PAM. Ow!

LEN. Oorr lovely!

He tickles her. She chokes.

This'll put 'airs on yer chest!

They try to laugh quietly. The door opens. HARRY *puts his head in. He goes out. He shuts the door.* LEN *calls:*

'Ave a toffee!

PAM. Oo-oo 'ave a toffee!

LEN. Tried that mint with the 'ole in it?

PAM. 'Ave a toffee!

LEN. What about the ol' dolly mixture? – Will 'e give yer a ruckin'?

PAM. Ain' got the nerve.

LEN (*calls*). Nosey ol' gander!

They laugh.

See 'is tongue 'angin' out?

PAM. 'E's fetchin' 'is dinner-box out the kitchen.

LEN (*calls*). Don't work too 'ard, mate!

PAM. Lay off, or 'e'll stay in out a spite.

LEN (*calls*). Take a toffee for tea break, Dad! – I'd like'a sleep round 'ere. Yer'd be lovely an' warm in the mornin'.

PAM. Yer're juss greedy!

LEN. I give yer 'alf the sweets!

PAM. I paid. Anyway, Mum'll be back.

LEN. O. That the front door?

PAM. Yeh.

She goes to the curtains.

'E's off.

LEN. Didn't take long.

PAM. I tol' yer.

LEN. Better be worth waitin' for.

PAM. Up to you, ain' it!

LEN. Thass all right then.

She comes to the sofa and starts to undo his belt.

This is the life.

SCENE TWO

Park.

PAM *and* LEN *in a rowing boat. Otherwise stage bare.*

LEN. Cold?

PAM. No.

LEN. Still pecky?

PAM. Yeh.

LEN. There's a bit'a choclit left. 'Ere.

PAM. No.

LEN. Go on.

PAM. Ta.

LEN. Thass yer lot.

PAM. Why?

LEN. No more.

Silence.

I still ain' paid me rent this week.

PAM. Me mum won't reckon that.

LEN. Ain' got round to it.

PAM. Surprised she ain' said.

Slight pause.

LEN. She ever let on?

PAM. 'Bout us?

LEN. Yeh.

PAM. No.

LEN. She don't mind?

PAM. Don't 'ave to. Your money comes in 'andy.

Silence.

LEN. She reckon me, yer reckon?

PAM. Never arst.

LEN. Thought she might'a said.

PAM. Never listen.

LEN. O.

PAM. Yer ain't spent it?

LEN. 'Er rent?

PAM. Yeh.

LEN. Nah!

PAM. Juss wondered.

LEN. Don' yer truss me?

PAM. I'm goin' a knit yer a jumper.

LEN. For me?

PAM. I ain' very quick.

LEN. Can't say I noticed.

PAM. Yer'll 'ave t'buy the wool.

LEN. Knew there'd be a catch.

PAM. I got a smashin' pattern.

LEN. You worried about that rent?

PAM. I 'ad it give us.

LEN. Yer 'adn't better be one of them naggers.

PAM. What colour's best?

LEN. Thass about one thing your ol' girl *don't* do.

PAM. What?

LEN. Nag 'er ol' man.

PAM. What's yer best colour?

LEN. They all suit me.
PAM. I like a red. Or a blue.
LEN. Anythin' bright.

Slight pause.

PAM. I 'ave t' 'ave an easy pattern.
LEN. Will it be ready for the 'oneymoon?
PAM. We ain' 'avin' 'oneymoon.
LEN. 'Oo's payin'?
PAM. You.
LEN. I can see I'll 'ave t' watch out.

Pause.

PAM. Whass the time?
LEN. Don't know.
PAM. Gettin' on.
LEN. Shouldn't wonder.
PAM. Where's the choclit?
LEN. Yer 'ad it all.
PAM. O.
LEN. Sorry.
PAM. There weren't much.
LEN. I'll get some when we go in.
PAM. I 'ad a blinkin' great dinner.
LEN. I reckon yer got a kid on the way.
PAM. I ain'.
LEN. Never know yer luck.
PAM. Yer'll 'ave t' get up early in the mornin' t' catch me.
LEN. Done me best.
PAM. Yer got a dirty mind.

Slight pause.

LEN. I'm 'andy with me 'ands. Yer know, fix up the ol'
decoratin' lark and knock up a few things. Yeh. We'll 'ave
a fair little place. I ain' livin' in no blinkin' sty.

PAM. Sounds all right.

LEN. Easy t' kep swep' out an' that. Yer'll be all right.

PAM. I'd better.

He puts his head in her lap. There is a slight pause.

LEN. 'S great 'ere.

Pause.

  Pam.

PAM. What?

LEN. Why did yer pick me up like that?

PAM. Why?

LEN. Yeh.

PAM. Sorry then?

LEN. Tell us.

PAM. 'Ow many girls you 'ad?

LEN. No, I tol' yer my life.

PAM. 'Old on.

LEN. What?

PAM. Yer got a spot.

LEN. Where?

PAM. 'Old still.

LEN. Is it big?

PAM. 'Old still.

LEN. Go easy!

PAM. Got it!

LEN. Ow!

She bursts a spot on his neck.

PAM. Give us yer 'anky.

LEN. Yer got it?

PAM. Yeh.

LEN. Ow! It d'narf 'urt.

He gives her his handkerchief. She dips her hand in the water and dries it on the handkerchief. She gives it back to him.

PAM. Yer wan'a wash sometimes.

LEN. Cheeky cow. (*Slight pause. They are both lying down.*)
   Yer wouldn't go back with any ol' sod?

PAM. You are rotten.

LEN. I'm sorry. Pam?

PAM. You're 'urtin' me leg.

LEN. I'm sorry.

PAM. No.

LEN. When yer goin' a start me jumper?

PAM (*still annoyed*). Why d'yer 'ave t' say that?

LEN. Tell us about me jumper.

PAM. Ain' got no wool.

LEN. I'll get it t'morra. An' we'll start lookin' for a place
   t'morra.

PAM. No places round 'ere.

LEN. Move out a bit. It's better out.

PAM. Yer'll be lucky.

LEN. Bin lucky with you. (*His head is in her lap. He twists so
   that he can put his arms round her.*) Ain' I bin lucky with you?

PAM. Yer don't deserve it.

LEN. I said I'm sorry – I won't arst no more. It's me good
   looks done it.

PAM. It *was* you. It weren't no one else.

LEN. Less go t'bed early t'night.

PAM. If yer go t' bed much earlier it won't be worth gettin' up.

LEN. Lovely. 'Ow about a sing-song.

PAM. No.

LEN (*sings*).

>   Be kind to'yer four-footed friends
>   That duck may be somebody's brother
>   Yer may think that this is the end
>   Well it is.

Slight pause.

   They must a' forgot us. We bin 'ere 'ours.

PAM. Do the rest.

LEN. Some mothers!

Pause.

Livin' like that must 'a got yer down.

PAM. Used to it.

LEN. They ought to be shot.

PAM: Why?

LEN. Don't it every worry yer?

PAM. Ow?

LEN. Supposed you turned out like that?

PAM. No.

LEN. 'Ow'd it start?

PAM. Never arst.

LEN. No one said?

PAM. Never listen. It's their life.

LEN. But –

PAM. Yer can't do nothin', yer know. No one'll thank yer.

LEN. 'Ow long's it bin goin' on?

PAM. Longer'n I know.

Pause. He sits and leans towards her.

LEN. Must a' bin bloody rotten when yer was a kid.

PAM. Never know'd no difference. They 'ad a boy in the war.

LEN. Theirs?

PAM. Yeh.

LEN. I ain't seen 'im.

PAM. Dead.

LEN. O.

PAM. A bomb in a park.

LEN. That what made 'em go funny?

PAM. No. I come after.

LEN. What a life.

PAM. I 'ad me moments.

LEN. I won't turn out like that. I wouldn't arst yer if I didn't know better 'n that. That sort of carry-on ain' fair.

PAM. I know.

LEN. We'll get on all right. I wonder it never sent yer off yer nut.

PAM. Yer don't notice.

LEN. It won't be long now. Why don't yer blow up an' knock their 'eads t'gether?

PAM (*shrugs*). I 'ope I never see 'em again. Thass all.

Slight pause. LEN *looks round.*

LEN. I ain' got a decent jumper.

Pause.

'Ow'd they manage?

PAM. When?

LEN. They writes notes or somethin'?

PAM. No.

LEN. 'Ow's that?

PAM. No need.

LEN. They must.

PAM. No.

LEN. Why?

PAM. Nothin' t' say. 'E puts 'er money over the fire every Friday, an' thass all there is. Talk about somethin' else.

LEN. Whass she say about 'im?

PAM. Nothin'.

LEN. But –

PAM. She never mentions 'im an' 'e never mentions 'er. I don' wanna talk about it.

LEN. They never mention each other?

PAM. I never 'eard 'em.

LEN. Not once?

PAM. *No!*

LEN. It's wet down 'ere.

Pause.

I ain' livin' with me in-laws, thass a fact.

FRED (*off*). Four!

LEN. I never got yer placed till I saw yer ol' people.

PAM. I never chose 'em!

LEN. I never meant that! –

PAM. Don't know why yer wan'a keep on about 'em!

LEN. – I never try an' get at yer!

FRED *comes on down right. His back to the audience.*

FRED. Number-four-bang-on-the-door!

PAM. Thass us.

FRED. Less 'ave yer!

LEN. Less stay out!

PAM. Why?

FRED. Oi!

PAM (*to* LEN). Come on.

LEN. We're a pirate ship.

FRED (*taking the micky*). You devil!

PAM. Yer'll 'ave t' pay.

LEN. Come an' get us!

FRED. Wass up darlin'? 'As 'e got 'is rudder stuck?

PAM (*to* LEN). I'm 'ungry.

LEN. Why didn't yer say?

LEN *starts to pull in.* FRED *moves towards them as the boat comes in.*

FRED. Lovely. 'Elp 'im darlin'. Thass lovely. She 'andles that like a duchess 'andles a navvy's pick.

LEN. All right?

FRED. Lovely.

He leans out and jerks the boat in. PAM *stands awkwardly.*

LEN. Steady.

FRED. 'Old tight, darlin'.

He lifts her out.

Yer wanna watch Captain Blood there. Very nice.

LEN. Okay?

PAM. Ta.

FRED. Very 'ow's yer father.

LEN (*stepping out*). Muddy.

PAM (*to* LEN). I enjoyed that.

FRED. Same 'ere.

LEN. We'll do it again.

FRED. Any time.

PAM (*to* LEN). Got everythin'?

FRED (*to* PAM). You 'ave.

LEN (*clowning*). Watch it!

FRED. 'Oo's bin' 'aving a bash on me duckboards?

PAM (*to* LEN). Less 'ave me bag.

FRED. Bashin's extra.

PAM. Yer wanna get yerself a job.

FRED. I got one.

PAM. 'Irin' out boats!

FRED. I'd rather 'ire you out, darlin'.

LEN (*joking*). Watch it!

PAM (*to* LEN). Ready?

LEN. Yeh.

LEN *and* PAM *start to go right.*

FRED. Why, you got a job for us? I wouldn't mind a bit a grind for you.

PAM. Yer'll 'ave t' join the union.

FRED. I'm in, love. Paid up.

LEN (*joking*). Yer'll be in the splash in a minute.

LEN *and* PAM *go out left.*

FRED (*to himself*). Right up. Like you, darlin'.

SCENE THREE

Park. Bare stage.

PETE, BARRY, MIKE, COLIN. PETE *wears a brown suit and suede shoes. The jacket is short in the seat and tight on the shoulders. His tie is black. The others wear jeans and shirts.*

MIKE. What time they bury the bugger?

PETE. Couldn't tell yer.

COLIN. Don' yer wan'a go?

PETE. Leave off! 'Oo's goin' a make me time up?

COLIN. Why yer goin' then?

PETE. The ol' lady'll ruck if I don't.

MIKE. Yeh, they reckon anythin' like this.

COLIN. Blinkin' morbid.

MIKE. Looks lovely in a black tie don' 'e!

They laugh.

PETE. What a carry on! 'E come runnin' round be'ind the bus. Only a nipper. Like a flash I thought right yer nasty bastard. Only ten or twelve. I jumps right down on me revver an' bang I got 'im on me off-side an' 'e shoots right out under this lorry comin' straight on.

MIKE. Crunch.

COLIN. Blood all over the shop.

MIKE. The Fall a the Roman Empire.

PETE. This lorry was doin' a ton in a built-up street.

BARRY. Garn! Yer never seen 'im.

PETE. No?

BARRY. 'It 'im before yer knew 'e was comin'.

PETE (*lighting his pipe*). Think I can't drive?

COLIN. What a giggle, though.

MIKE. Accidents is legal.

COLIN. Can't touch yer.

PETE. This coroner-twit says 'e's sorry for troublin' me.

MIKE. The law thanks 'im for 'is 'elp.

PETE. They paid me for comin'.

MIKE. An' the nip's mother reckons 'e ain' got a blame 'isself.

COLIN. She'll turn up at the funeral.

PETE. Rraammmmmmmmmm!

COLIN. Bad for the body work.

MIKE. Can't yer claim insurance?

PETE. No.

MIKE. Choked!

COLIN. Ruined 'is paint work.

BARRY. 'E's 'avin' yer on!

MIKE. Yer creep.

COLIN. Yer big creep.

PETE. Let 'im alone. 'E don't know no better.

COLIN. 'E don't know nothin'.

MIKE. Big stingy creep.

COLIN. Yer wouldn't 'ave the guts.

BARRY. No guts?

MIKE. Yeh.

BARRY. Me?

COLIN. Not yer grannie.

BARRY. I done blokes in.

MIKE. 'Ere we go.

BARRY. More'n you 'ad 'ot dinners. In the jungle. Shootin'
    up the yeller-niggers. An' cut 'em up after with the ol'
    pig-sticker. Yeh.

MIKE (*hoots*).

COLIN. Do leave off!

BARRY. You lot wouldn't know a stiff if it sat up and shook
    'ands with yer!

MIKE. Aa! Shootin' up the yeller-nigs!

COLIN. Sounds like brothers a your'n.

BARRY. Get stuffed!

PETE (*to them all*). Chuck it, eh?

COLIN. Yeller-niggers! My life! What yer scratchin'?

MIKE. 'E's got a dose.

PETE. Ain' surprisin'.

COLIN. Ain' it dropped off yet?

MIKE. Tied on with a ol' johnny.

COLIN. It's 'is girl.

MIKE. 'Is what?

PETE. Gunged-up ol' boot.

COLIN. 'E knocked it off in the back a 'is car last night –
MIKE. 'Is what?
PETE. Pile a ol' scrap.
MIKE. Ought a be put off the road.
COLIN. 'E was knockin' it off in the back an' –
MIKE. I 'eard.
PETE. What?
MIKE. The back-bumper fell off.
PETE. Yeh?
COLIN. I's a fact!
PETE. My life!
MIKE. An' what she say?
COLIN. Yer juss drop somethin'.
BARRY. Bollocks!

He laughs at himself.

MIKE. Yeh!
COLIN. 'Aving trouble with yer 'orn?
BARRY. It weren't no bumper! Me fog lamp come off.
MIKE. 'Is fog lamp!

They roar with laughter.

COLIN. I knew somethin' come off!
MIKE. Flippin' fog lamp!
PETE. Thass what she calls it!
COLIN. Wonder it weren't 'is engine come out.
BARRY. Better'n nothin'.
MIKE. Yer couldn't knock someone down with that!
PETE. It'd come t' a stop.
MIKE. Shootin' up the yeller-niggers!
BARRY. Yeh, yer ain' lived!

LEN *comes on down right.*

PETE. Me mum's got a dirty great wreath.
MIKE. Yeh!

COLIN. Give somethin' for it?
PETE. I ain' a 'ippocrit.
COLIN. Oi – whass-yer-name!
LEN. Eh?
COLIN. It's – Lenny, ain' it?
LEN. Yeh. – O! 'Ow's it goin', admiral?
COLIN. 'Ow's yerself?
LEN. Not so dodgy. Long time.
COLIN. Me and 'im was t'school t'gether.
MIKE. Yeh?
COLIN. What yer bin doin'?
BARRY. Reform school?
MIKE. Don't 'e show yer up!
COLIN. Take no notice. Creep! – Workin'?
LEN. Worse luck.
COLIN. I couldn't place yer for a minute. (*Slight pause.*) Yeh.
LEN. Yer ain' changed much.
BARRY. What yer doin' now?
LEN. Waitin'.
MIKE. I – I!
COLIN. It was in the park, yer 'onour!
MIKE. This girl come up t'me.
COLIN. An' drags me in the bushes.
BARRY. Yer 'onour.

He laughs.

COLIN. I knew she was thirteen.
MIKE. But she twisted me arm.
COLIN. An' 'er ol' dad 'd bin bashin' it off for years.
BARRY. Yer 'onour.

He laughs.

COLIN. Twisted yer what?
MIKE. Never know yer luck!
COLIN. Married?

LEN. Gettin' ready.

BARRY. 'Oo with?

LEN. We're waitin' –

COLIN. Pull the other one!

MIKE. What for?

PETE. Till she drops 'er nipper.

COLIN. Else it looks bad goin' up the aisle.

MIKE. She can 'ide it be'ind 'er flowers.

BARRY. Is that what they carry 'em for?

COLIN. We live an' learn.

MIKE. Takes all sorts.

MARY *comes on up right.*

LEN. Thass us.

COLIN. *That?*

LEN *goes to* MARY.

PETE. One man's meat.

MIKE. More like scrag-end.

BARRY. Bit past it, ain' she?

PETE. She's still got the regulation 'oles.

MIKE. Experience 'elps. Yer get a surprise sometimes.

LEN (*to* MARY). Less give yer a 'and.

MARY. Whew! Ta.

She gives him the shopping bags.

LEN. Okay?

MARY. I was juss goin' ter drop 'em.

MIKE. 'Ear that.

BARRY. Goin' a drop 'em!

COLIN. In the park?

MIKE. At 'alf-past twelve?

PETE (*laughing*). The dirty ol' scrubber.

LEN *and* MARY *start to cross left.*

BARRY (*to* COLIN). That what they taught yer at school?

COLIN *whistles.*

LEN (*amused*). Put a sock in it.

BARRY. What yer got at the top a your legs? What time's breakfast?

MARY. That your mates?

LEN. They're juss 'avin' a laugh.

MARY. You all right with them bags?

LEN. Yeh.

COLIN. Roger the lodger 'ad a bad cough.

MIKE. 'E sneezed so 'ard.

COLIN. 'Is door knob fell off.

BARRY. 'Is landlady said we'll soon 'ave yer well.

COLIN. So she pulled off 'er drawers.

MIKE. An' polished 'is bell!

MARY. Lot a roughs.

LEN *and* MARY *go out left.*

PETE. Makes yer think.

COLIN. What?

PETE. Never know what yer missin'.

MIKE. True.

PETE. I knew a bloke once reckoned 'e knocked off 'is grannie.

COLIN. Yeh?

PETE. All a mistake.

COLIN. 'Ow's that?

PETE. There was a power cut at the time an' –

BARRY. – 'E thought it was 'is sister.

PETE. Ain' yer clever!

MIKE. Trust the unions!

COLIN. Makes yer think, though.

BARRY *blows a raspberry.*

PETE (*smoking his pipe*). Never know 'alf what goes on.

MIKE. That age she must be 'angin' out for it.

PETE. Stuffin' it all in before it's too late.

COLIN. Yeh.

There is a slight pause.

PETE. Ooorrr! I'll 'ave t' fix up a little bird t'night. 'Ere, wass the time?

COLIN. Time we're back t' work.

They groan.

MIKE (*to* PETE). Time yer're round the church they'll 'ave 'im down the 'ole or up the chimney or wherever 'e's goin'.

PETE. I reckon they wanna put 'im down the 'ole an' ꝑ the chain.

SCENE FOUR

The living room. Dark.

The door opens. MARY *comes in. She puts on the light.* HARRY *is sitting in the armchair. He is partly asleep.* MARY *puts sauce, salt and pepper on the table and goes out.* HARRY *gets up. He goes to the door and puts the light out. He goes back to the armchair. Pause.*

The door opens. MARY *comes in. She puts on the light. She takes knife, fork, spoon and table napkin to the table. She lays the napkin as a small table cloth. The door opens.* PAM *comes in. She wears a slip and carries a hair brush and cosmetics. She switches on the TV set.* MARY *goes out. Without waiting to adjust the set* PAM *goes to the couch and sits. She makes up her face. The door opens.* MARY *comes in with a plate of food.*

MARY (*calls*). It's on the table.

She walks towards the table. To PAM.

I told you not to walk round like that.

MARY *puts the food on the table and goes out.* PAM *goes to the TV set and adjusts it. She goes back to the couch and sits. She makes up her face.* MARY *comes in.*

(*At the door*). It's on the table! That's the second time!

She goes to the TV set.

I don't know 'ow they 'ave the nerve to put it on.

She switches to another channel. She steps back to look at the picture. She steps forward to adjust it. She steps back.

Hm.

She steps forward and adjusts it again.

If yer put it in the oven it goes 'ard as nails.

She steps back and looks at the set. She goes to the couch, sits and watches TV. Pause.

PAM. More like one a them daft mirrors at a circus.
MARY. The man'll 'ave to come an' fix it.

She goes to the set and adjusts it.

You don't know 'ow to switch it on. It goes all right when I do it.

LEN *comes in.*

LEN. Smells great.
MARY. You've let it ruin.
LEN. Nah.
MARY. Cold as Christmas.
LEN. Do me.

He sits at the table and eats.

MARY (*goes to the set and re-adjusts it*). I don't know. – Did yer put the light out in the scullery?
LEN. Yeh.

MARY. We need a new one. That's what's wrong with it.

She goes back to the couch and sits. She watches silently. Pause.

PAM. Looks like one a them black an' white minstrels.
MARY. Well you do it, an' don't sit there pokin' 'oles.
PAM. I ain' watchin'.
MARY. Sounds like it.

LEN *eats.* MARY *watches.* PAM *makes up.* HARRY *is still. The TV is fairly loud. A very long pause.*
   Slowly a baby starts to cry. It goes on crying without a break until the end of the scene. Nothing happens until it has cried a long while. Then MARY *speaks.*

   Can yer see?
LEN. Yeh.
MARY. Move yer seat.
LEN. I can see.

Pause.

   Yer a fair ol' cook.
MARY. It's ruined. Yer get no encouragement t' try.

Pause. The baby screams with rage. After a while MARY *lifts her head in the direction of the screams.*

   Pam-laa!

Slight pause. PAM *stands and puts her cosmetics in a little bag. She goes to the TV set. She turns up the volume. She goes back to the couch and sits.*

   There's plenty of left-overs.
LEN. Full up.
MARY. An' there's rhubarb and custard.
LEN: O.

Pause. The baby chokes.

PAM. Too lazy t' get up an' fetch it.

MARY. Don't start. Let's 'ave a bit a peace for one night.

Pause.

PAM. 'Is last servant died a over-work.

LEN. I ain' finished this, nosey.

MARY. Why don't yer shut that kid up.

PAM. I can't.

MARY. Yer don't try.

PAM. Juss cries louder when I go near it.

MARY (*watching TV*). I ain' goin' up for yer. (*Still watching TV.*) High time it 'ad a father. (*To* LEN). There's plenty a tea in the pot.

LEN (*watching TV*). Yeh.

MARY (*watching TV*). That's what it needs. No wonder it cries. (*Pause. To* LEN.) Busy?

LEN. Murder.

MARY (*watching TV*). Weather don't 'elp.

LEN (*still watching TV*). Eh? (*The baby whimpers pitifully. Pause. Still watching TV.*) Ha!

Pause. PAM *picks up her things and goes out.*

MARY. About time.

LEN. Wan'a cup?

MARY. No. There's milk in that custard. It'll only get thrown out.

LEN (*stands*). I'll bust.

He goes out.

MARY (*calls*). On the top shelf.

LEN (*off*). What?

MARY. It's on the top shelf!

Pause. LEN *comes in. He carries a plate to the table.*

Did yer get it?

LEN. Yeh.

He sits.

MARY. Shut that door, Len. Me 'ead's playin' me up again.
LEN. Take some a yer anadins.
MARY. I've 'ad too many t'day. Thass what makes it worse.

LEN *goes back to the door and shuts it. He goes to the table and eats.*

Did yer put the oven out?
LEN. An' the light.
MARY. I ain' made a money, y'know.

Suddenly the baby cries much louder.

Put some sugar on it.

LEN *sprinkles the sugar from a teaspoon.*

People'll send the police round 'ere next.
LEN. It'll cry itself t'sleep.

PAM *comes in. She wears a dress.*

MARY. It's still cryin'.
PAM. I thought the cat was stuck up the chimney.

She sits on the couch and pulls up her stockings.

'Ad a good look? – I'm tired a 'im watchin' me all the time.
MARY. I told yer t' get dressed in the scullery like anybody else.
PAM. I can dress where I like in me own 'ome.
LEN (*to himself*). O no.
PAM. You say somethin'?
LEN (*calmly*). Yeh – shut up.
PAM. I suppose that's your idea a good manners.

Pause.

When yer leavin' us? I'm sick an' tired a arstin'.

MARY. I don't wanna 'ear all this again t'night.

PAM. 'E gets on me nerves.

LEN. I ain' leavin' that kid.

PAM. Why?

LEN. With you?

PAM. It ain' your kid.

LEN. No?

PAM. Yer'll 'ave t' take my word for it.

LEN. Yer don't even know when you're lyin'.

Pause. The baby cries.

PAM. I don't understan' yer. Yer ain' got no self respect.

LEN. You 'ave like.

PAM. No one with any self respect wouldn't wanna stay.

LEN *pours tea for himself.*

Yer'll 'ave t'go sometime. Yer can't juss 'ang on till yer rot.

MARY. Pack it up! No wonder that kid cries!

PAM. Why don't you tell 'im t' go? It's your job. 'E's gettin' on me nerves every night. If it goes on much longer I'll be ill.

MARY. That'll teach yer t'bring fellas back.

PAM (*to* HARRY). Why don't you tell im? It's your 'ouse. There's bin nothin' but rows an' arguments ever since 'e got 'ere. I've 'ad all I can stand! (*Slight pause.*) Dad!

HARRY. I ain' gettin' involved. Bound t'be wrong.

PAM (*to* LEN). I don't understan' yer. Yer can't enjoy stayin' 'ere.

LEN *drinks his tea.*

It's bad enough bein' stuck with a kid without 'avin' you 'anging roun' me neck. The 'ole street's laughin' be'ind yer back.

LEN. I ain' leavin' that kid.
PAM. Take it.
LEN. With me?
PAM. 'Ow else?
MARY. 'Ow can 'e?
PAM. Thass 'is worry.
MARY. 'E can't look after a kid.
PAM. Put it on the council.
MARY (*shrugs*). They wouldn't 'ave it if they've got any sense.

The baby cries.

PAM. Well?
LEN. Kids need proper 'omes.
PAM. Yer see!
LEN (*looks in the teapot*). Out a' water.

He goes out.

MARY. Wouldn't yer miss it?
PAM. That racket?

The baby whimpers. There is a ring. PAM *goes out.* MARY *quickly tidies the couch.* LEN *comes back with the teapot.*

MARY. Did the door go?
LEN (*nods*). Juss then.
FRED (*off*). All right, all right. I said I'm sorry, ain' I?

PAM *is heard indistinctly.*

  Well let's say 'allo first!

FRED *comes in.*

  'Evenin'. 'Evenin', ma.
MARY. We're just watchin' telly.
FRED. Anythin' interestin'?
MARY. Come in.
FRED. 'Lo, Len. 'Ow's life?
LEN. Usual. 'Ow's the job?

FRED. Don't talk about it.

PAM *comes in.*

PAM. I still don't see 'ow that makes yer all this late.

FRED. Give it a rest, Pam.

PAM. The same last time.

MARY. Take yer coat off.

PAM. Yer oughta let me know if yer're goin'a be late.

FRED. 'Ow could I? Sorry love. We'll juss 'ave t' make it later in future.

PAM (*to* MARY). Can I put the kid in your room?

MARY. No wonder it can't sleep. Pushed around like some ol' door mat.

PAM. Can I or can't I? I ain' sittin' there with that row goin' on.

MARY. Do what yer like.

FRED (*to* PAM). Got plenty a fags?

MARY. Yer will anyway.

PAM (*to* FRED). Ready?

FRED. See yer, Lenny boy.

LEN. Yeh.

PAM. It's all the same if I was meetin' yer outside in the street. I'd be left standin' in the cold.

FRED (*following* PAM *to the door*). Got any fags? I left mine be'ind.

PAM *and* FRED *go out.* LEN *stacks the things on the table and takes some of them out. The baby's crying suddenly gets louder.* LEN *comes in again. He picks up the sauce and the table napkin and goes out.* MARY *turns off the TV set and goes out.* HARRY *goes to the table and pours himself tea.* LEN *comes back.*

LEN. O.

HARRY. Finished.

LEN. Ta.

Pause.

Wish t'God I could take that kid out a this.

HARRY (*drinks*). Better.

LEN. No life growin' up 'ere.

HARRY (*wipes his mouth on the back of his hand*). Ah.

LEN. Wish t' God I 'ad some place.

HARRY. Yer wan'a keep yer door shut.

LEN. What?

HARRY. T'night.

LEN. Me door?

HARRY. Yer always keep yer door open when 'e's sleepin' with 'er.

LEN. I listen out for the kid. They ain' bothered.

MARY (*off*). Night, Len.

LEN (*calls*). Night. (*To* HARRY.) More?

HARRY. No.

LEN. Plenty in the pot.

HARRY (*wipes his mouth on the back of his hand*). Yer'll catch cold with it open.

LEN (*holding the teapot*). Night, then.

He goes to the door.

HARRY (*sitting in the armchair*). Put that light out.

LEN *puts the light out and goes. The crying sobs away to silence.*

SCENE FIVE

LEN's *bedroom. It is shaped like the living-room. Furniture: a single bed up right, a wooden chair close to it.* PAM *is in bed.* LEN *stands centre, away from her.*

LEN. Did yer take yer medicine?

Pause.

Feelin' better?

PAM. I'm movin' down t' me own room t'morra. Yer'll 'ave t' move back up 'ere.

LEN. Quieter up 'ere.

PAM. Like a blinkin' grave.

LEN. Why don't yer 'ave the telly up?

PAM. No.

LEN. Easy fix a plug.

PAM. Did yer see Fred?

LEN. Yer never took yer medicine. (*He pours her medicine and gives it to her.*) 'Ere. (PAM *takes it.*) Say ta. (*She drinks it and gives a small genuine* 'Ugh!') Read yer magazines?

PAM. Did Fred say anythin'?

MARY (*off*). Pam-laa! She gettin' up, Len?

PAM (*to herself*). O God.

MARY (*off*). The doctor says there's nothin' t' stop yer gettin' up. Yer're as well as I am.

LEN *closes the door but the voice is still heard.*

Pam-laa! The dinner's on the table.

LEN. Yer better off up 'ere out a 'er way.

PAM. The cow.

LEN *straightens the bed.*

Leave that.

LEN. You're comin' undone.

PAM. Leave it.

LEN. It's all –

PAM. I said leave it!

LEN (*continuing*). Someone's got a give yer a 'and.

PAM. I won't 'ave yer pullin' me about.

LEN (*walking away*). Why don't yer sit in a chair for 'alf 'our?

PAM. Mind yer own business.

LEN. Yer ain't doin' yerself no good lyin' there.

MARY (*off*). She gettin' up?

LEN. I'm only tryin' a 'elp.

PAM. Don't want yer 'elp.

LEN. Yer got bugger all idea 'ow to look after yerself.

PAM. Go away.

LEN. Some one –

PAM. For Ch⁻issake!

LEN. Someone's got a stick up for yer. (*Slight pause.*) Yer
treated me like dirt. But I ain't goin' a carry on like that.

MARY (*off*). Pamm-laa!

PAM (*calls*). Shut up! I'm sick a' the lot of yer! (*Slight pause.*)
Shut up!

LEN *goes out.*

PAM. Thank Chriss for that.

MARY (*off*). She up yet?

LEN *answers indistinctly. Pause.* PAM *pulls out the blankets that*
LEN *tucked in.* LEN *comes back with the baby.*

LEN (*to baby*). 'Ello then! 'Ello then!

PAM. O no.

LEN. Look-ee that. 'Oo that mummy-there?

PAM. She's got the grub out on the table.

LEN. It'll keep.

PAM. She ain' better row me out for it.

LEN. Take it.

PAM. Put it back.

LEN. Yer ought a take it.

PAM. Don't keep tellin' me what I ought a do.

LEN. Yer ain' even looked at it for weeks.

PAM. Ain' going to.

LEN. Yer'd feel better.

Pause.

'Ello then.

PAM. Did yer give 'im what I wrote?

LEN. 'E's busy, 'e reckons. It's 'is busy time.

PAM. Ha!

LEN. 'Avin' yourn on a tray?

PAM. If yer like.

LEN. It knows yer voice.

PAM. Put it away before it starts.

LEN. Good for its lungs.

PAM. Yer d'narf annoy me, Len.

LEN. I know.

PAM. Yer're always pesterin' me.

LEN. Someone's got a look after yer.

PAM. There yer are! Thass another annoyin' thing t' say. (*She sits.*) This dump gives me the 'ump. Put that away.

LEN. Yer can't let it lie on its back all day. Someone's got a pick it up.

PAM (*sitting back*). Why should I worry? Its father don't give a damn. I could be dyin' an' 'e can't find ten minutes.

LEN. I'm blowed if I'm goin' a put meself out if yer can't co-operate.

He tries to put the baby in her arms.

PAM. I tol' yer take it back! Get off a me! Yer bloody lunatic! Bleedin' cheek! (*Calls.*) Mum!

LEN. You 'ave it for a change!

He puts the baby on the bed.

PAM. Yer goin' mad! It's fallin'. Catch it!

LEN *puts the baby so that it is safe.*

LEN. I ain' your paid nurse!

PAM (*calls*). Mum! – I know why Fred ain' come – yer bin tearin' up me letters.

LEN. 'E did!

PAM. Yer little liar! (*She turns away from the baby.*) I ain' touchin' it.

LEN. It'll stay there all night!

PAM. Thass what yer call 'elpin' me.

Pause. LEN *picks up the baby.*

See!

LEN. Can't give it a cold juss because we're rowin'.

He goes towards the door. He stops.

'E said 'e'd look in.

PAM (*she turns round*). When? (*She turns back to the wall.*) What did 'e say?

LEN. I said yer wanted to see 'im. 'E goes 'e's up to 'is eyes in it. So I said I got a couple of tickets for Crystal Palace. 'E's knockin' off early.

PAM. Saturday?

LEN. T'night.

PAM (*turns*). Yer got 'im downstairs!

LEN. No.

PAM (*calls*). Mum – is Fred there? Fred? – 'E might be early.

LEN. There's a good 'alf 'our yet.

PAM (*excited*). I 'ope 'is lot wins.

LEN. 'E might be late.

PAM. Not for football. Yer can say she's upstairs if yer wan' a go. Put it like that.

LEN (*looks at child*). 'E's well away.

PAM. I ain' cut me nails all the time I bin in bed.

MARY (*off*). Lennie!

LEN. Shall I get the scissors?

PAM. She won't shut up till yer go down. I got me own.

MARY (*off*). Leonard! I keep callin' yer. (*Outside the door.*) 'Ow many more times. (*She comes in.*) I bin callin' the last 'alf 'our. Dinner won't be fit t'eat.

LEN. Juss puttin' the nipper back.

MARY. That's the last time I cook a 'ot meal in this 'ouse. I mean it this time. (*To* PAM.) Yer can make yer own bed

t'morra, you. (*To* LEN.) I ain' sweatin' over a 'ot stove.
No one offers t'buy me a new one. (*To* PAM.) I can't afford
t' keep yer on yer national 'ealth no longer. I'm the one 'oo
ought to be in bed.

MARY *goes out.*

PAM. I got all patches under me eyes.
LEN. No.
PAM. I feel awful.
LEN. Yer look nice.
PAM. I'll 'ave t' 'ave a wash.
LEN. Yeh.

SCENE SIX

The Park. A bare stage. FRED *holds a fishing-rod out over the
stalls. He wears jeans and an old dull leather jacket.* LEN *sits
beside him on a small tin box. On the ground there are a bait
box, odds and ends box, float box, milk bottle, sugar bottle, flask
and net.*

LEN. Round our place t'night?
FRED. No.
LEN. It's Saturday.
FRED. O yeh.
LEN. She won't like it.
FRED. No.

Pause.

Yer wan' a get yerself a good rod.
LEN. Can't afford it.

FRED. Suit yerself.

LEN. Lend us yourn.

FRED. Get knotted.

Slight pause.

LEN. I in yer way then?

FRED. Eh?

LEN. Sittin' 'ere.

FRED. Free country.

LEN. Yer'd never think it.

FRED. Nippy.

LEN. Lend us yer jacket.

FRED. Jump in.

LEN. 'Ow much yer give for that?

FRED. Yer get 'em on h.p.

LEN. Fair bit a work.

FRED (*runs his hand along the rod*). Comes in 'andy.

Pause.

LEN. She said yer was comin' round for the telly.

FRED. News t' me.

LEN. Don't know whass on.

FRED. Don't care.

LEN. Never looked. (*Slight pause.*) Never bothers me. Easy find out from the paper if yer –

FRED. Don't keep on about it.

LEN. Eh?

FRED. Don't bloody well keep on about it.

LEN. Suits me. (*Slight pause.*) I was agreein' with yer. I thought like –

FRED. Oi – Len, I come out for the fishin'. I don't wanna 'ear all your ol' crap.

Slight pause. LEN *turns his head right and stares at the river.*

'Onest, Len – yer d'narf go on.

LEN. I only said I was agreein' with yer. Blimey, if yer can't ...

He stops. Pause.

FRED. Sod!
LEN. Whass up?
FRED. Bait's gone.
LEN. Gone? They've 'ad it away.
FRED. Never.
LEN. Must 'ave.
FRED. More like wriggled off.
LEN. I mounted it 'ow yer said.
FRED (*winds in*). Come 'ere. Look.

He takes a worm from the worm box.

Right, yer take yer worm. Yer roll it in yer 'and t' knock it out. Thass first. Then yer break a bit off. Cop 'old o' that.

He gives part of the worm to LEN.

LEN. Ta.
FRED. Now yer thread yer 'ook through this bit. Push it up on yer gut. Leave it. – Give us that bit. Ta. Yer thread yer other bit on the 'ook, but yer leave a fair bit 'angin' off like that, why, t'wriggle in the water. Then yer push yer top bit down off the gut and camer-flarge yer shank. Got it?
LEN. Thass 'ow I done it.
FRED. Yeh. Main thing, keep it neat.

He casts. The line hums.

Lovely.

A long silence.

The life.

Silence.

LEN. Down the labour Monday.

FRED *grunts*.

Start somethin'.

Silence.

No life, broke.

FRED. True.

Silence. LEN *pokes in the worm box with a stick.*

Feed 'em on milk.

LEN. Fact?

Silence.

I'll tell 'er yer ain' comin'.

FRED. Len!

LEN. Well yer got a let 'er know.

FRED. 'Oo says?

LEN. Yer can't juss –

FRED. Well?

LEN. Shut up a minute.

FRED. Listen, mate, shut yer trap an' give us a snout.

LEN. No.

FRED. Yer're loaded.

LEN. Scroungin' git! Smoke yer own. – She'll be up 'alf the night. That'll be great. – I reckon yer got a bloody nerve takin' my fags, yer know I'm broke. – Yer believe in keepin' em waitin' for it.

Slight pause.

FRED. Yer used to knock 'er off, that right?

LEN. Once.

FRED. There yer are then.

LEN. What?

FRED. It's all yourn.

LEN. She don't wan'a know.

FRED. 'Ow's that?

LEN. Since you 'ad 'er.

FRED. What d'yer expect? No – they're like that. Once they go off, they go right off.

LEN. Don't even get a feel.

FRED. 'Appens all the time. Give us a snout.

LEN. No.

FRED. Tight arse.

Slight pause.

LEN. Skip?

FRED. Yeh?

LEN. What yer reckon on 'er?

FRED. For a lay?

LEN. Yeh.

FRED. Fair. Depends on the bloke.

LEN. Well?

FRED. No – get that any time.

Silence.

LEN. Gettin' dark.

Silence.

FRED. Call it a day.

LEN. In a minute.

FRED. Never know why yer stick that dump.

LEN. Seen worse.

FRED. I ain'.

Slight pause.

LEN. Skip?

FRED. Whass up now?

LEN. Why's she go for you?

FRED. They all do mate.

LEN. No, why's she – ill over it?

FRED. Come off it, she 'ad a drop a the ol' flu.

LEN. Yeh. But why's she like that?

FRED. It ain' me money.

LEN. They all want the same thing, I reckon. So you must 'ave more a it.

FRED. Thass true! Oi!

LEN. What?

FRED. Still.

Pause.

Thought I 'ad a touch.

Pause.

Nah.

They ease off. FRED *looks up at the sky.*

Jack it in.

LEN. Anyway, thass what they reckon.

FRED. Eh?

LEN. They all want the same thing.

FRED. O.

LEN. I reckon yer're 'avin' me on.

FRED. Me?

LEN. Like the fish that got away.

FRED. I ain' with yer.

He shakes his head.

LEN. That big! (*He holds his hands eighteen inches apart.*)

FRED (*laughs*). More like that! (*He holds his hands three feet apart.*)

LEN. Ha! Thass why she's sick.

FRED. Now give us a fag.

LEN. No.

FRED (*spits*). 'Ave t' light one a me own.

He takes one of his own cigarettes from a packet in his breast pocket. He does not take the packet from the pocket.

LEN. Mind the moths.

FRED. Yer ever 'ad worms up yer nose, in yer ears, an' down yer throat?

LEN. Not lately.

FRED. Yer will in a minute.

LEN. Well give us a snout then.

FRED. Slimey ponce!

He gives LEN *a cigarette.* LEN *gives* FRED *a light.*

LEN. I used a 'ear, know that?

FRED. 'Ear what? – 'E's like a flippin' riddle.

LEN. You an' 'er.

FRED. Me an' 'oo?

LEN. On the bash.

FRED. Do what?

LEN. Straight up.

FRED. Chriss.

LEN. Yeh.

FRED. Yer kiddin'.

LEN. On my life. Kep me up 'alf the night. Yer must a bin trying for the cup.

FRED (*draws his cigarette*). Why didn't yer let on?

LEN. No, it's all a giggle, ain't it?

FRED (*shrugs*). Yeh? Makes yer feel a right charlie.

He drops his cigarette on the floor and treads on it.

Chriss. Thass one good reason for jackin' 'er in.

LEN. Don't start blamin' me.

FRED. An' you was listenin'?

LEN. Couldn't 'elp it.

FRED. O.

He lays his rod on the ground and crouches to pack his things.

Yer didn't mind me goin' round 'er's.

LEN. Same if I did.
FRED. I didn't know like.
LEN. Yer never ruddy thought. Any'ow, I don't mind.
FRED. I thought she was goin' spare.
LEN. Wan'a 'and?
FRED. No. Give us that tin.

He packs in silence.

I reckon it was up t' you t' say. Yer got a tongue in yer
'ead.

Silence. MIKE *comes in. He has a haversack slung from one
shoulder and carries a rod. He wears a small, flashy hat.*

FRED. No luck?
MIKE. Wouldn't feed a cat.
LEN. Waste a time.
MIKE. Same 'ere.
FRED. Got a breeze up.
MIKE. What yer doin'?
FRED. Now?
MIKE. Yeh, t'night.
FRED. Reckon anythin'?
MIKE. Bit a fun.
FRED. Suits me.
MIKE. You're on.
FRED. Up the other end?
MIKE. 'Ow's the cash?
FRED. Broke. You?
MIKE. I'll touch up the ol' lady.
FRED. Get a couple for me.
LEN. That'll pay the fares.
MIKE. Pick yer up roun' your place.
FRED. Not too early. 'Ave a bath first.
MIKE. Never know 'oo yer'll be sleepin' with.
FRED. After eight.

MIKE. I feel juss right for it.

LEN. What?

MIKE. Out on the 'unt.

FRED (*imitates a bullet*). Tschewwwwww!

MIKE. 'E picks 'em up at a 'undred yards.

FRED. It's me magnetic cobblers.

PAM *comes in. She pushes the pram. The hood is up. A long blue sausage balloon floats from a corner of the hood.*

PAM. 'Ello.

FRED. Whass up?

PAM. Out for a walk.

MIKE (*nods at pram*). Bit late for that, ain' it?

PAM (*to* FRED). What yer got?

FRED. Nothin'.

PAM (*tries to look*). Less 'ave a look.

FRED. Nothin' for you!

PAM. Keep yer shirt on.

MIKE. Yer nearly missed us.

PAM (*to* FRED). Don't get so 'airy-ated.

MIKE. We was juss off.

FRED. What yer cartin' that about for?

PAM. Felt like a walk.

FRED. Bit late.

PAM. Why?

FRED. That ought a be in bed.

PAM. Fresh air won't kill it.

FRED. Should a done it earlier.

PAM. Never 'ad time. Why didn't you?

FRED. You know best.

PAM. When yer comin' round?

FRED. I'll look in.

PAM. When?

FRED. I don't know.

PAM. When about?

FRED. Later on.

PAM. Shall I get somethin' to eat?

FRED. No.

PAM. No bother.

FRED. The ol' lady'll 'ave it all set up.

PAM. I got two nice chops.

FRED. Shame.

PAM. Well see 'ow yer feel. There's no one in now. I got rid a 'em.

FRED. Pity yer didn't say.

PAM. What time then?

FRED. I'll be there.

PAM. Sure?

FRED. Yeh.

PAM. Say so if yer ain'.

FRED. I'll be there.

PAM. That means yer won't.

FRED. Up t'you.

PAM. Why don't yer say so?

FRED (*picks up his gear. To* MIKE). Thass the lot.

PAM. It ain' no fun waitin' in all night for nothin'.

MIKE. Ready?

FRED (*takes a look round*). Yeh.

PAM. Why can't yer tell the truth for once?

FRED. Fair enough. I ain' comin'.

LEN. Pam –

PAM. Yer 'ad no intention a comin'.

LEN. Yer left the brake off again.

MIKE (*to* FRED). Okay?

PAM (*to* LEN). Put it on, clever.

FRED (*to* MIKE). Yeh.

PAM (*to* FRED). I knew all along.

FRED. Come on, Pam. Go 'ome.

PAM. Fred.

FRED. I know.

PAM. I didn't mean t' go off. I was goin' a be nice, I still ain' better.

FRED. Go 'ome an' get in the warm. It's late.

LEN (*putting on the brake*). Yer wan' a be more careful.

PAM (*to* FRED). It's my fault. I never stop t'think.

FRED. Yer wan' a stop thinkin' about yerself, I know that.

PAM. It's them pills they give me.

MIKE (*to* FRED). You comin' or ain' yer.

FRED. Yeh.

PAM. No.

FRED. I'll come round one night next week.

PAM. No.

FRED. Monday night. Ow's that?

PAM. Yer'll change yer mind.

FRED. Straight from work.

PAM. Yer said that before.

FRED. It's the best I can offer.

PAM. I can't go back there now.

FRED. Yer'll be okay.

PAM. If I sit on me own in that room another night I'll go round the bend.

FRED. Yer got the kid.

PAM. Juss t'night. I couldn't stand it on me own no more. I 'ad a come out. I don't know what I'm doin'. That kid ought a be in bed. Less take it 'ome, Fred. It's 'ad new-moanier once.

FRED. You take it 'ome.

PAM. Juss this last time? I won't arst no more. I'll get mum t' stay in with me.

FRED. It's no use.

PAM. Yer ain' seen it in a long time, 'ave yer?

She turns the pram round.

It's puttin' on weight.

FRED. Eh?

PAM. It don't cry like it used to. Not all the time.

MIKE. Past carin'.

PAM. Doo-dee-doo-dee. Say da-daa.

FRED. Yeh, lovely.

He looks away.

LEN (*looking at the baby*). Blind.

PAM (*to* LEN). Like a top.

FRED. What yer give it?

PAM. Asprins.

FRED. That all right?

PAM. Won't wake up till t'morra. It won't disturb yer. What time'll I see yer?

FRED. I'll look in. I ain' sayin' definite.

PAM. I don't mind. Long as I know yer're comin'.

FRED. All right.

PAM. Pity t' waste the chops. I think I'll do 'em in case –

FRED. Yeh, right. It's all accordin'.

PAM. I'll wait up.

FRED. It'll be late, see.

PAM. Thass all right.

FRED. Pam.

PAM. I'll treat meself t' box a choclits.

FRED. There's plenty a blokes knockin' about. Why don't yer pick on someone else.

PAM. No.

MIKE. Yer can 'ave me, darlin'. But yer'll 'ave t' learn a bit more respect.

PAM. 'Ow can I get out with that 'angin' round me neck? 'Oo's goin' a look at me?

FRED. Yer ol' girl'll take it off yer 'ands.

MIKE. Drop 'er a few bob.

FRED. Yer don't try.

PAM. I can't!

FRED. Yer'll 'ave to.

PAM. I can't! I ain' goin' to!

FRED. I ain' goin' a see yer no more.

PAM. No.

FRED. We got a sort this out some time.

PAM. Yer promised!

FRED. It's a waste a time!

PAM. *They* 'eard!

FRED. No.

MIKE. Come on, mate.

FRED. It's finished.

MIKE. Thank Chriss. Less shift!

PAM. Juss t'night. I don't care if yer bin with yer girls. Come 'ome after. Juss once. I won't bother yer. I'll let yer sleep. Please.

FRED. Chriss.

PAM. O what d'you care? I was flat on me back three bloody weeks! 'Oo lifted a finger? I could a bin dyin'! No one!

She starts pushing the pram.

MIKE. Good riddance!

PAM (*stops*). You're that kid's father! Yeh! Yer ain't wrigglin' out a that!

FRED. Prove it.

PAM. I *know*!

FRED. You *know*?

MIKE. Chriss.

FRED. 'Alf the bloody manor's bin through you.

PAM. Rotten liar!

FRED. Yeh?

To MIKE. Ain' you 'ad 'er?

MIKE. Not yet.

FRED. Yer'll be next.

Points to LEN.

What about 'im?

To LEN. Eh?

To MIKE. Your's must be the only stiff outside the church-yard she ain' knocked off.

PAM. I 'ate you!

FRED. Now we're gettin' somewhere.

PAM. Pig!

FRED. Thass better. Now piss off!

PAM. I will.

MIKE. Ta-ta!

PAM. An' yer can take yer bloody bastard round yer tart's! Tell 'er it's a present from me!

PAM *goes out. She leaves the pram.*

MIKE. Lovely start t' the evenin's entertainment.

FRED (*calls*). I ain' takin' it! It'll bloody stay 'ere!

MIKE. What yer wan'a let 'er get away with –

FRED. Don't you start! I 'ad enough with 'er!

LEN. I'd better go after 'er.

FRED. Send 'er back.

LEN. See 'ow she is.

LEN *goes out after* PAM.

FRED (*calls*). Don't leave 'er kid. Take it with yer.

MIKE *whistles after her.* FRED *throws his gear down.*

Lumbered!

MIKE. 'E'll send 'er back.

FRED. 'E ain' got the gumption. We'll drop it in on the way back.

MIKE. Leave it 'ere. Won't be worth goin' time we're ready.

FRED. Give it five minutes.

MIKE. Yer won't see 'er again.

FRED. That won't be the worst thing in me life.

MIKE. Can't yer arst your Liz t' look after it?

FRED. She'd tear me eyes out.

Pause. They sit.

MIKE. They opened that new church on the corner.

FRED. What?

MIKE. They got a club.

FRED. O yeh.

MIKE. We'll 'ave a quick little case round.

FRED. T'night?

MIKE. Yeh.

FRED. Get stuffed.

MIKE. Straight up.

FRED. Pull the other one.

MIKE. Best place out for'n easy pick up.

FRED. Since when?

MIKE. I done it before. There's little pieces all over the shop, nothin' a do.

FRED. Fact?

MIKE. The ol' bleeder shuts 'is eyes for prayers an' they're touchin' 'em up all over the place. Then the law raided this one an' they 'ad it shut down.

FRED. Do leave off.

PETE *and* COLIN *come in right.*

PETE. 'Ow's it then?

MIKE. Buggered up.

COLIN. Like your arse.

MIKE. Like your flippin' ear in a minute.

PETE. I – I!

COLIN. Wass on t'night?

MIKE. Laugh.

BARRY *comes in after* PETE *and* COLIN.

BARRY. Fishin'?

FRED. 'Angin' the Chrissmas decorations.

BARRY. 'Oo's bin chuckin' big dog ends?

MIKE. Where?

BARRY. 'Ardly bin lit.

PETE. 'E's juss waitin' for us t'shift an' 'e'll be on it.

FRED (*holds it out*). On the 'ouse.

MIKE. 'As 'e got a little tin?

COLIN. Like'n ol' tramp?

BARRY. O yeh – 'oo's mindin' the baby?

COLIN (*seeing pram*). Wass that for?

MIKE. Pushin' the spuds in.

FRED (*flicks the dog end to* BARRY). Catch!

COLIN. 'Oo left it 'ere?

BARRY. 'E's takin' it for a walk.

PETE. Nice.

FRED. Piss off.

BARRY. We don't wan' the little nipper t'ear that! Oi, come
  'ere.

COLIN *and* PETE *go to the pram.*

  Oo's 'e look like?

They laugh.

MIKE. Don't stick your ugly mug in its face!

PETE. It'll crap itself t' death.

BARRY. Dad'll change its nappies.

COLIN (*amused*). Bloody nutter!

FRED. You wake it up an' yer can put it t'sleep.

COLIN *and* PETE *laugh.*

BARRY. Put it t'sleep?

COLIN. 'E'll put it t'sleep for good.

PETE. With a brick.

MIKE. 'E don't care if it's awake all night.

BARRY. 'Oo don't? I'm like a bloody uncle t' the kids round
  our way. (*He pushes the pram.*) Doo-dee-doo-dee-doo-dee

MIKE (*to* FRED). Jack it in eh?

FRED. Give 'er another minute.

MIKE. We should a made Len stay with it.

FRED. Slipped up. 'E dodged off bloody sharpish.

MIKE. Sly bleeder.

FRED. I don't know – bloody women!

MIKE. Know a better way?

FRED *and* MIKE *are sitting down left.* PETE *and* COLIN *are right.* BARRY *pushes the pram.*

BARRY.
> Rock a bye baby on a tree top
> When the wind blows the cradle will rock
> When the bough breaks the cradle will fall
> And down will come baby and cradle and tree
>   an' bash its little brains out an' dad'll scoop
>   'em up and use 'em for bait.

They laugh.

FRED. Save money.

BARRY *takes the balloon. He poses with it.*

COLIN. Thought they was pink now.

BARRY (*pokes at* COLIN's *head*). Come t' the pictures t'night darlin'? (*He bends it.*) It's got a bend in it.

MIKE. Don't take after its dad.

BARRY (*blows it up*). Ow's that then?

COLIN. Go easy.

BARRY (*blows again*). Thass more like it. (*Blows again.*)

COLIN. Do leave off.

MIKE. That reminds me I said I'd meet the girl t'night.

BARRY *blows. The balloon bursts.*

COLIN. Got me!

He falls dead. BARRY *pushes the pram over him.*

Get off! I'll 'ave a new suit out a you.

BARRY (*pushing the pram round*). Off the same barrer?

PETE. Ain' seen you 'ere before, darlin'.

BARRY. 'Op it!

PETE. 'Ow about poppin' in the bushes?

COLIN. Two's up.

BARRY. What about the nipper?

PETE. Too young for me.

He 'touches' BARRY.

BARRY. 'Ere! Dirty bastard!

He projects the pram viciously after COLIN. It hits PETE.

PETE. Bastard!

PETE and BARRY look at each other. PETE gets ready to push the pram back – but plays at keeping BARRY guessing. MIKE and FRED are heard talking in their corner.

MIKE. If there's nothin' in the church, know what?

FRED. No.

MIKE. Do the all-night laundries.

FRED. Yer got a 'and it to yer for tryin'.

MIKE. Yer get all them little 'ousewives there.

FRED. Bit past it though.

MIKE. Yeh, but all right.

PETE pushes the pram violently at BARRY. He catches it straight on the flat of his boot and sends it back with the utmost ferocity. PETE sidesteps. COLIN stops it.

PETE. Stupid git!

COLIN. Wass up with 'im?

BARRY. Keep yer dirty 'ands off me!

PETE. 'E'll 'ave the little perisher out!

BARRY. O yeh? An' 'oo reckoned they run a kid down?

PETE. Thass different.

BARRY. Yeh – no one t' see yer.

PETE pulls the pram from COLIN, spins it round and pushes it violently at BARRY. BARRY sidesteps and catches it by the handle as it goes past.

BARRY. Oi – oi!

He looks in the pram.

COLIN. Wass up?

COLIN *and* PETE *come over.*

It can't open its eyes.
BARRY. Yer woke it.
PETE. Look at its fists.
COLIN. Yeh.
PETE. It's tryin' a clout 'im.
COLIN. Don't blame it.
PETE. Goin' a be a boxer.
BARRY. Is it a girl?
PETE. Yer wouldn't know the difference.
BARRY. 'Ow d'yer get 'em t'sleep?
PETE. Pull their 'air.
COLIN. Eh?
PETE. Like that.

He pulls its hair.

COLIN. That 'urt.

They laugh.

MIKE. Wass 'e doin'?
COLIN. Pullin' its 'air.
FRED. 'E'll 'ave its ol' woman after 'im.
MIKE. Poor sod.
BARRY. 'E's showin' off.
COLIN. 'E wants the coroner's medal.
MIKE (*comes to the pram*). Less see yer do it.

PETE *pulls its hair.*

O yeh.
BARRY. It don't say nothin'.
COLIN. Little bleeder's 'alf dead a fright.

MIKE. Still awake.
PETE. Ain' co-operatin'.
BARRY. Try a pinch.
MIKE. That ought a work.
BARRY. Like this.

He pinches the baby.

COLIN. Look at that mouth.
BARRY. Flippin' yawn.
PETE. Least it's tryin'.
MIKE. Pull its drawers off.
COLIN. Yeh!
MIKE. Less case its ol' crutch.
PETE. Ha!
BARRY. Yeh!

He throws the nappy in the air.

    Yippee!
COLIN. Look at that!

They laugh.

MIKE. Look at its little legs goin'.
COLIN. Ain' they ugly!
BARRY. Ugh!
MIKE. Can't keep 'em still!
PETE. 'Avin' a fit.
BARRY. It's dirty.

They groan.

COLIN. 'Old its nose.
MIKE. Thass for 'iccups.
BARRY. Gob its crutch.

He spits.

MIKE. Yeh!
COLIN. Ha!

He spits.

MIKE. Got it!
PETE. Give it a punch.
MIKE. Yeh less!
COLIN. There's no one about!

PETE *punches it.*

 Ugh! Mind yer don't 'urt it.
MIKE. Yer can't.
BARRY. Not at that age.
MIKE. Course yer can't, no feelin's.
PETE. Like animals.
MIKE. 'It it again.
COLIN. I can't see!
BARRY. 'Arder.
PETE. Yeh.
BARRY. Like that!

He hits it.

COLIN. An' that!

He also hits it.

MIKE. What a giggle!
PETE. Cloutin's good for 'em. I read it.
BARRY (*to* FRED). Why don't you clout it?
FRED. It ain' mine.
PETE. Sherker. Yer got a do yer duty.
FRED. Ain' my worry. Serves 'er right.
BARRY. 'Ere, can I piss on it?
COLIN. Gungy bastard!
MIKE. Got any matches?

They laugh.

PETE. Couldn't yer break them little fingers easy though?
COLIN. Snap!
PETE. Know what they used a do?

MIKE. Yeh.

PETE. Smother 'em.

BARRY. Yeh. That'd be somethin'.

COLIN. Looks like a yeller-nigger.

BARRY. 'Onk like a yid.

FRED. Leave it alone.

PETE. Why?

FRED. Yer don't wan' a row.

PETE. What row?

MIKE. What kid?

COLIN. I ain' seen no kid.

BARRY. Not me!

PETE. Yer wouldn't grass on yer muckers?

FRED. Grow up.

BARRY. D'narf look ill. Stupid bastard.

He jerks the pram violently.

PETE. Thass 'ow they 'ang yer – give yer a jerk.

MIKE. Reckon it'll grow up an idiot.

PETE. Or deformed.

BARRY. Look where it come from.

PETE. Little bleeder.

He jerks the pram violently.

That knocked the grin off its face.

MIKE. Look! Ugh!

BARRY. Look!

COLIN. What?

They all groan.

PETE. Rub the little bastard's face in it!

BARRY. Yeh!

PETE. Less 'ave it!

He rubs the baby. They all groan.

BARRY. Less 'ave a go! I always wan'ed a do that!

PETE. Ain' yer done it before?

BARRY *does it. He laughs.*

COLIN. It's all in its eyes.

Silence.

FRED. There'll be a row.
MIKE. It can't talk.
PETE. 'Oo cares?
FRED. I tol' yer.
COLIN. Shut up.
BARRY. I noticed 'e ain' touched it.
COLIN. Too bloody windy.
FRED. Yeh?
PETE. Less see yer.
BARRY. Yeh.
PETE. 'Fraid she'll ruck yer.
FRED. Ha!

He looks in the pram.

Chriss.
PETE. Less see yer chuck that.

PETE *throws a stone to* FRED. FRED *doesn't try to catch it. It falls on the ground.* COLIN *picks it up and gives it to* FRED.

MIKE (*quietly*). Reckon it's all right?
COLIN (*quietly*). No one around.
PETE (*quietly*). They don't know it's us.
MIKE (*quietly*). She left it.
BARRY. It's done now.
PETE (*quietly*). Yer can do what yer like.
BARRY. Might as well enjoy ourselves.
PETE (*quietly*). Yer don't get a chance like this everyday.

FRED *throws the stone.*

COLIN. Missed.
PETE. That ain't'!

He throws a stone.

BARRY. Or that!

He throws a stone.

MIKE. Yeh!
COLIN (*running round*). Where's all the stones?
MIKE (*also running round*). Stick it up the fair!
PETE. Liven 'Ampstead 'eath! Three throws a quid! Make a
  packet.
MIKE (*throws a stone*). Ouch!
COLIN. 'Ear that?
BARRY. Give us some.

He takes stones from COLIN.

COLIN (*throws a stone*). Right in the lug 'ole.

FRED *looks for a stone.*

PETE. Get its 'ooter.
BARRY. An' its slasher!
FRED (*picks up a stone, spits on it*). For luck, the sod.

He throws.

BARRY. Yyooowwww!
MIKE. 'Ear it plonk!

A bell rings.

MIKE. 'Oo's got the matches?

He finds some in his pocket.

BARRY. What yer doin'?
COLIN. Wan'a buck up!
MIKE. Keep a look out.

He starts to throw burning matches in the pram. BARRY *throws a stone. It just misses* MIKE.

Look out, yer bleedin' git!
COLIN. Guy Fawkes!
PETE. Bloody nutter! Put that out!
MIKE. No! You 'ad what you want!
PETE. Yer'll 'ave the ol' bloody park 'ere!

A bell rings.

BARRY. Piss on it! Piss on it!
COLIN. Gungy slasher.
MIKE. Call the R.S.P.C.A.

A bell rings.

FRED. They'll shut the gates.
PETE (*going*). There's an 'ole in the railin's.
BARRY. 'Old on.

He looks for a stone.

PETE. Leave it!
BARRY. Juss this one!

He throws a stone as PETE *pushes him over. It goes wide.*

Bastard!
To PETE. Yer put me off!
PETE. I'll throttle yer!
BARRY. I got a get it once more!

The others have gone up left. He takes a stone from the pram and throws it at point blank range. Hits.

Yar!

COLIN. Where's this 'ole!
MIKE. Yer bleedin' gear!
FRED. Chriss.

He runs down to the rod and boxes. He picks them up.

BARRY. Bleedin' little sod!

He hacks into the pram. He goes up left.

PETE. Come on!

A bell rings. FRED *has difficulty with the boxes and rod. He throws a box away.*

FRED. 'Ang on!

He goes up left.
They go off up left, making a curious buzzing. A long pause.
PAM *comes in down left.*

PAM. I might a know'd they'd a left yer. Lucky yer got someone t' look after yer. Muggins 'ere.

She starts to push the pram. She does not look into it. She speaks in a sing-song voice, loudly but to herself.

'Oo's 'ad yer balloon. Thass a present from grannie. Goin' a keep me up 'alf the night? Go t' sleepies. Soon be 'ome. Nice an' warm, then. No one else wants yer. Nice an' warm. Soon be 'omies.

SCENE SEVEN

A cell. Left centre a box to sit on. Otherwise, the stage is bare.
A steel door bangs. FRED *comes in from the left. He has a mack over his head. He sits on the case. After a slight pause he takes off the mack.*

Silence. A steel door bangs. PAM *comes in left.*

PAM. What 'appened?
FRED. Didn't yer see 'em?
PAM. I 'eard.

FRED. Bloody 'eathens. Thumpin' and kickin' the van.

PAM. Oo?

FRED. Bloody 'ousewives! 'Oo else? Ought a be stood up an' shot!

PAM. You all right?

FRED. No. I tol' this copper don't open the door. He goes we're 'ere, the thick bastard, an' lets 'em in. Kickin' an' punchin'.

He holds up the mack.

Look at it! Gob all over.

He throws it away from him.

'Course I ain' all right!

Mimicking her. 'Are yer all right?'

PAM. They said I shouldn't be 'ere. But 'e was ever so nice. Said five minutes wouldn't matter.

FRED. Right bloody mess.

PAM. They can't get in 'ere.

FRED. I can't get out there!

PAM. I ain't blamin' yer.

FRED. Blamin' me? Yer got bugger all t'blame me for, mate! Yer ruined my life, thass all!

PAM. I never meant –

FRED. Why the bloody 'ell bring the little perisher out that time a night?

PAM (*fingers at her mouth*). I wanted a –

FRED. Yer got no right chasin' after me with a pram! Drop me right in it!

PAM. I was scared t' stay –

FRED. Never know why yer 'ad the little bleeder in the first place! Yer don't know 'what yer doin'! Yer're a bloody menace!

PAM. Wass it like?

FRED. They wan' a put you in, then yer'll find out. Bring any burn?

PAM. No.

FRED. Yer don't think a nothin'! Ain' yer got juss one?

PAM. No.

FRED. Yer're bloody useless.

PAM. What'll 'appen!

FRED. 'Ow do I know? I'll be the last one a know. The 'ole thing was an accident. Lot a roughs. Never seen 'em before. Don't arst me. Blokes like that anywhere. I tried to chase 'em off.

PAM. Will they believe that?

FRED. No. If I was ten years older I'd get a medal. With a crowd like our'n they got a knock someone. (*He goes right.*) Right bloody mess.

PAM. Yer never bin in trouble before. Juss one or two woundin's an' that.

FRED. 'Alf murdered with a lot a 'and bags!

PAM. Yer wan' a arst t' see the doctor.

FRED. Doctor! They shouldn't let him touch a sick rat with a barge pole. (*He walks a few steps.*) It's supposed a be grub. A starvin' cat 'ld walk away. (*He walks a few more steps.*) Wass bin 'appening?

PAM. Don't know.

FRED. On yer own?

PAM. What about them others?

FRED. What about 'em?

PAM. I could say I saw 'em.

FRED. That'd make it worse. Don't worry. I'm thinkin' it all out. This way they don't know what 'appened. Not definite. Why couldn't I bin tryin' a 'elp the kid? I got no cause t' 'arm it.

He sits on the box.

PAM. I tol' 'em.

FRED (*he puts his arms round her waist and leans his head against her*). Yer'll 'ave t' send us letters.

PAM. I'm buyin' a pad on me way 'ome.

FRED. Pam. I don't know what'll 'appen. There's bloody gangs like that roamin' everywhere. The bloody police don't do their job.

PAM. I'll kill meself if they touch yer.

A steel door bangs. LEN *comes in left.*

I tol' yer t' wait outside.

LEN. I got 'im some fags. (*To* FRED.) I 'ad a drop 'em 'alf.

PAM. 'E still won't leave me alone, Fred.

LEN. I only got a minute. They're arstin' for a remand.

FRED. Chriss. That bloody mob still outside?

LEN. They've 'emmed 'em off over the road.

FRED. Bit bloody late.

PAM. Tell 'im t' go.

LEN. We both got a go. That inspector wants you.

FRED. Where's the snout?

LEN. Put it in yer pocket.

FRED (*to* PAM). See yer after.

She puts her arms round him before he can take the cigarettes.

PAM. I'll wait for yer.

FRED (*pats her back*). Yeh, yeh. God 'elp us.

LEN (*to* PAM). Yer'll get 'im into trouble if yer don't go.

FRED *nods at* PAM. *She goes out crying.*

FRED. 'Ow many yer got?

LEN. Sixty. I 'ad a drop 'em 'alf.

FRED. Will it be all right?

LEN. Give 'em a few like, an' don't flash 'em around.

FRED. She never 'ad none. I'll do the same for you sometime.

LEN. Put 'em in yer pocket.

FRED. I don't know what I'll get.

LEN. Manslaughter. (*Shrugs.*) Anythin'.

FRED. It was only a kid.

LEN. I saw.

FRED. What?

LEN. I come back when I couldn't find 'er.

FRED. Yer ain't grassed?

LEN. No.

FRED. O.

LEN. I was in the trees. I saw the pram.

FRED. Yeh.

LEN. I saw the lot.

FRED. Yeh.

LEN. I didn't know what t'do. Well, I should a stopped yer.

FRED. Too late now.

LEN. I juss saw.

FRED. Yer saw! Yer saw! Wass the good a that? That don't 'elp me. I'll be out in that bloody dock in a minute!

LEN. Nothin'. They got the pram in court.

FRED. Okay, okay. Reckon there's time for a quick burn?

LEN. About.

He gives FRED *a light.*

INTERVAL

SCENE EIGHT

The living-room.

HARRY *irons,* LEN *sits.*

LEN. Yer make a fair ol' job a that.

Pause.

   Don't yer get choked off?

HARRY. What?

LEN. That every Friday night.
HARRY. Got a keep clean.
LEN. Suppose so.

Pause.

  Yer get used t' it.
HARRY. Trained to it in the army.
LEN. O.
HARRY. Makes a man a yer.

MARY *comes in. She looks around.*

MARY *to* LEN. I wish yer wouldn't sit around in yer ol' work-
  clothes an' shoes. Yer got some nice slippers.

MARY *goes out.*

LEN. She won't let Pam.
HARRY. Eh?
LEN. She won't let Pam do that for yer.
HARRY. Don't take me long.

Long pause.

LEN. Yer could stop 'er money.

Slight pause.

  Then she couldn't interfere.
HARRY. Don't take long. Once yer get started.
LEN. Why don't yer try that?
HARRY. That Pam can't iron. She'd ruin 'em.
LEN. Ever thought a movin' on?
HARRY. This stuff gets dry easy.
LEN. Yer ought a think about it.
HARRY. Yer don't know what yer talking about, lad.
LEN. No. I don't.
HARRY. It's like everthin' else.
LEN. 'Ow long yer bin 'ere?

HARRY. Don't know. (*He stretches his back. He irons again.*)
Yer mate's comin' out.

LEN. Yeh. Why?

HARRY. Pam's mate. (*He spits on the iron.*) None a it ain'
simple.

LEN. Yer lost a little boy eh?

HARRY. Next week, ain't it?

LEN. I got a shirt yer can do. (*Laughs.*) Any offers?

HARRY. She meet 'im?

LEN. Ain' arst.

HARRY. You?

LEN (*shrugs*). I'd 'ave t' get time off.

HARRY. O.

LEN. 'Ow d'yer get on at work?

HARRY (*looks up*). It's a job.

LEN. I meant with the blokes?

HARRY (*irons*). They're all right.

LEN. Funny, nightwork.

PAM *comes in. She has her hair in a towel. She carries a portable
radio. Someone is talking. She sits on the couch and finds a
pop programme. She tunes in badly. She interrupts this from
time to time to rub her hair.*

LEN (*to* HARRY). 'Ow about doin' my shirt?

He laughs. PAM *finishes tuning. She looks round.*

PAM. 'Oo's got my *Radio Times*? You 'ad it?

HARRY *doesn't answer. She turns to* LEN.

You?

LEN (*mumbles*). Not again.

PAM. You speakin' t' me?

LEN. I'm sick t' death a yer bloody *Radio Times*.

PAM. Someone's 'ad it. (*She rubs her hair vigorously.*) I ain'
goin' a get it no more. Not after last week. I'll cancel it.
It's the last time I bring it in this 'ouse. I don't see why I

'ave t' go on paying for it. Yer must think I'm made a money. It's never 'ere when I wan'a see it. Not once. It's always the same. (*She rubs her hair.*) I notice no one else offers t' pay for it. Always Charlie. It's 'appened once too often this time.

LEN. Every bloody week the same!

PAM (*to* HARRY). Sure yer ain' got it?

HARRY. I bought this shirt over eight years ago.

PAM. That cost me sixpence a week. You reckon that up over a year. Yer must think I was born yesterday.

Pause. She rubs her hair.

Wasn't 'ere last week. Never 'ere. Got legs.

She goes to the door and shouts.

Mum! She 'eard all right.

She goes back to the couch and sits. She rubs her hair.

Someone's got it. I shouldn't think the people next door come in an' took it. Everyone 'as the benefit a it 'cept me. It's always the same. I'll know what t' do in future. Two can play at that game. I ain' blinkin' daft. (*She rubs her hair.*) I never begrudge no one borrowin' it, but yer'd think they'd have enough manners t' put it back.

Pause.

She rubs her hair.

Juss walk all over yer. Well it ain' goin' a 'appen again. They treat you like a door mat. All take and no give. Touch somethin' a their'n an' they go through the bloody ceilin'. It's bin the same ever since –

LEN. I tol' yer t' keep it in yer room!

PAM. Now yer got a lock things up in yer own 'ouse.

LEN. Why should we put up with this week after week juss because yer too –

PAM. Yer know what yer can do.

LEN. Thass yer answer t' everythin'.

PAM. Got a better one?

HARRY. They was a pair first off. Set me back a quid each. Up the market. One's gone 'ome, went at the cuffs. Worth a quid.

LEN. Chriss.

Pause.

PAM. I mean it this time. I'm goin' in that shop first thing Saturday mornin' an' tell 'im t' cancel it. I ain' throwin' my money down the drain juss to –

LEN. Wrap up!

PAM. Don't tell me what t' do!

LEN. Wrap up!

PAM. Thass typical a you.
She goes to the door and calls. Mum!
To LEN. I ain' stupid. I know 'oo's got it.
Calls. Mum! – She can 'ear.

HARRY. Ain' worth readin' any'ow.

LEN. Don't start 'er off again.

PAM (*to* LEN). You ain' sittin' on it, a course!

LEN. No.

PAM. Yer ain' looked.

LEN. Ain' goin' to.

PAM. 'Ow d'yer know yer ain' sittin' on it?

LEN. I ain' sittin' on it.

PAM (*to* HARRY). Tell 'im t' get up!

HARRY. Waste a good money.

PAM (*to* LEN). Yer'll be sorry for this.

LEN. I'll be sorry for a lot a things.

HARRY. Cuffs goin' on this one.

PAM (*by* LEN's *chair*). I ain' goin' till yer move.

HARRY. Lot a lies an' pictures a nancies.

PAM. Yer dead spiteful when yer wan'a be.

LEN. Thass right.

PAM (*goes to the couch, rubbing her hair*). 'E'oo laughs last. Fred's coming 'ome next week.

LEN. 'Ome?

PAM. 'Is ol' lady won't 'ave 'im in the 'ouse.

LEN. Where's 'e goin'?

PAM. Yer'll see.

LEN. 'E ain' 'avin' my room.

PAM. 'Oo said?

LEN. She won't let yer.

PAM. We'll see.

LEN. Yer ain' even arst 'er.

PAM. O no?

LEN. No.

PAM (*rubs her hair*). We'll see.

LEN. I'll 'ave one or two things t' say. Yer too fond a pushin' people about.

PAM. Must take after you.

LEN. I thought 'e'd be sharin' your room.

PAM. I ain' rowin' about it. 'E'll 'ave t' 'ave somewhere t' come out to. Chriss knows what it's like shut up in them places. It'll be nice an' clean 'ere for 'im when yer're gone.

LEN. 'Ave yer arst 'im yet?

PAM. I ain' rowin' about it. If 'e goes wanderin' off 'e'll only end up in trouble again. I ain' goin' a be messed around over this! We ain' gettin' any younger. 'E's bound a be different. (*She rubs her hair.*) Yer can't say anythin' in letters. Yer can't expect 'im to.

LEN. 'Ave yer arst 'im.

PAM. I don' wan' a talk about it.

LEN. You meetin' 'im?

PAM. Why? – You ain' comin'!

LEN. 'Oo said?

PAM. 'E don't want you there!

LEN. 'Ow d'yer know?

PAM. O let me alone!

LEN. 'E's my mate, ain' 'e?

PAM. I'm sick t' death a you under me feet all the time! Ain'
yer got no friends t' go to! What about yer people? Won't
they take yer in either?

LEN. Yer arst some stupid questions at times.

PAM. Yer can't 'ave no pride. Yer wouldn't catch me 'angin'
round where I ain' wanted.

LEN. 'Oo ain' wanted?

PAM. I don't want yer! They don't want yer! It's only common
sense! I don't know why yer can't see it. It's nothin' but rows
an' arguments.

LEN. 'Oo's fault's that?

PAM. Anybody else wouldn't stay if yer paid 'em! Yer caused
all the trouble last time.

LEN. I knew that was comin'.

PAM. None a that 'ld a 'appened if yer ain' bin 'ere. Yer never
give 'im a chance.

LEN. Yeh, yeh.

PAM. Yer live on trouble!

LEN. That ain' what 'e told everyone.

PAM. Same ol' lies.

LEN. Listen 'oo's talkin'!

PAM. Yer start off gettin' 'im put away –

LEN. Don't be bloody stupid!

PAM. Jealous! An' now 'e's comin' out yer still can't let 'im
alone!

LEN. *You* can't leave 'im alone yer mean!

PAM. Yer laughed yer 'ead off when they took 'im away.

LEN. Bloody stupid! You arst 'im!

PAM. Comin' 'ere an' workin' me up!

LEN. Yer wan'a listen t' yerself!

PAM. So do you.

LEN. Shoutin'.

PAM. 'Oo's shoutin'?

LEN. You are!

PAM. Yer 'ave t' shout with you!

LEN. Thass right!

PAM. Yer so bloody dense!

LEN. Go on!

PAM. Yer 'ave t' shout!

LEN. Yer silly bloody cow!

PAM. Shoutin' 'e says! 'Ark at 'im! 'Ark at 'im!

LEN. Shut up!

PAM. We ain' carryin' on like this! Yer got a stop upsettin'
me night after night!

LEN. You start it!

PAM. It's got a stop! It ain' worth it! Juss round an' round.

A very long silence.

Yer can't say it's the kid keepin' yer.

A long silence.

It certainly ain' me. Thass well past.

Silence.

Yer sit there in yer dirty ol' work clothes. (*To* HARRY.)
Why don't yer turn 'im out? Dad.

HARRY. 'E pays 'is rent.

PAM. Fred'll pay.

HARRY. 'As 'e got a job?

PAM. 'E'll get one.

HARRY. Will 'e keep it?

PAM. Thass right!

LEN. Now 'oo's startin' it?

PAM. You are.

LEN. I ain' said a word.

PAM. No – but yer sat there!

LEN. I got some rights yer know!

PAM. Yer're juss like a kid.

LEN. I'm glad I ain' yourn.

PAM. I wouldn't like t' 'ave your spiteful nature.

LEN. I certainly wouldn't like yourn!

PAM. Thass right! I know why yer sittin' there!

LEN. Yer know a sight bloody too much!

PAM. I know where my *Radio Times* is!

LEN. Stick yer bloody *Radio Times*!

PAM. I know why yer sittin' there!

LEN. That bloody paper!

PAM. Why don't yer stand up?

LEN. Yer don't even want the bloody paper!

PAM. As long as yer causin' trouble –

LEN. Yer juss wan' a row!

PAM. – then yer're 'appy!

LEN. If yer found it yer'd lose somethin' else!

PAM (*goes to* LEN's *chair*). Stand up then!

LEN. No!

PAM. Can't it a got there accidentally?

LEN. No!

PAM. Yer see!

LEN. I ain' bein' pushed around.

PAM. Yer see!

LEN. Yer come too much a it!

PAM. No yer'd rather stay stuck!

LEN. A sight bloody too much!

PAM. An' row!

LEN. Shut up!

PAM. Thass right!

LEN. I tol' yer t' shut up!

PAM. Go on!

LEN. Or I'll bloody well shut yer up!

PAM. O yeh!

LEN. Yer need a bloody good beltin'.

PAM. Touch me!

LEN. You started this!

PAM. Go on!

LEN (*he turns away*). Yer make me sick!

PAM. Yeh – yer see. Yer make me sick!

She goes to the door.

I ain' lettin' a bloody little weed like you push me around!
Calls. Mum.

She comes back.

I wish I 'ad a record a when yer first come 'ere. Butter
wouldn't melt in yer mouth.

Calls. Mum!

HARRY (*finishing ironing*). Thass that, thank Chriss.

PAM (*calls*). Mum! – She can' 'ear.

Calls. You 'eard?

HARRY. Put the wood in the 'ole.

LEN. I'd like t' 'ear what they're sayin' next door.

PAM. Let 'em say!

LEN. 'Ole bloody neighbour'ood must know!

PAM. Good – let 'em know what yer're like!

LEN. 'Oo wen' on about pride?

PAM (*calls through door*). I know yer can' ear.

MARY (*off*). You callin' Pam?

PAM (*to* LEN). One thing, anythin' else goes wrong I'll know
'oo t' blame.

MARY (*off*). Pam!

PAM. Let 'er wait.

MARY (*off*.) Pam!

LEN (*calls*). It's all right! One a 'er fits!

PAM (*calls*). 'E's sittin' on the chair.

MARY (*off*). What?

PAM (*calls*). 'E's got my paper!

MARY (*off*). What chair?

PAM (*calls*). 'E 'as!

MARY (*off*). I ain' got yer paper!

PAM (*calls*). It don't matter!

MARY (*off*). What paper's that?

PAM (*calls*). It don't matter! You bloody deaf?

LEN. Now start on 'er!

HARRY (*piling his clothes neatly*). Didn't take long.

PAM (*to* LEN). Yer're so bloody clever!

LEN. If I upset yer like this why don't *you* go?

PAM. Thass what you want!

LEN (*shrugs*). You want *me* t' go!

PAM. I ain' bein' pushed out on no streets.

LEN. I'm tryin' t' 'elp.

PAM. Yer wouldn't 'elp a cryin' baby.

LEN. Yer're the last one a bring that up!

PAM. 'Elp? – after the way yer carried on t'night.

LEN. I lost me job stayin' out a 'elp you when yer was sick!

PAM. Sacked for bein' bloody lazy!

LEN (*stands*). Satisfied?

PAM (*without looking at the chair*). Yer torn it up or burnt it!
  Wouldn't put that pass yer!

PAM *goes out. Silence.* HARRY *finishes folding his clothes.*

MARY (*off*). Found it yet?

Pause.

HARRY. Wan'a use it?

LEN. No.

HARRY *folds the board.*

SCENE NINE

The living-room.
LEN *has spread a paper on the floor. He cleans his shoes on it.*
MARY *comes in. She is in her slip. She walks about getting ready.*

MARY. 'Ope yer don't mind me like this.

LEN. You kiddin'?

MARY. It's such a rush. I don't really wan'a go.

LEN. Don't then.

MARY. I said I would now.

LEN. Say yer don't feel up to it.

MARY. Yes. (*She goes on getting ready.*) Makes a change I suppose.

LEN. Never know, it might be a laugh.

MARY. Yer got a do somethin' t' entertain yerself.

Pause.

I 'ope yer ain' usin' 'er *Radio Times*.

LEN. Ha!

MARY. She's got no patience. It'll land 'er in trouble one a these days. Look at that pram. I told 'er t'wait. She should a got two 'undred for that.

LEN. Easy.

MARY (*looks at her shoes*). This ain' nice. No, she 'as t' let it go for fifty quid, the first time she's arst. Can't be told. Yer couldn't give these a little touch up for me?

LEN. Sling 'em over.

MARY. Ta, dear.

LEN. What yer put on these?

MARY. That white stuff.

LEN *polishes her shoes in silence.*

Thinkin'?

LEN. No.

MARY. Whass worryin' yer?

LEN. Nothin'.

MARY. I expect yer're like me. Yer enjoy the quiet. I don't enjoy all this noise yer get.

LEN. She said somethin' about my room?

MARY (*amused*). Why?

LEN. What she say?

MARY. That worried yer?

LEN. I ain' worried.

MARY. She's not tellin' me 'ow t' run my 'ouse.

She pulls on her stockings.

LEN. O. (*Holds up her shoes.*) Do yer?

MARY. Very nice. Juss go over the backs dear. I like t' feel nice be'ind. I tol' 'er there's enough t' put up with without lookin' for trouble.

LEN. Better?

MARY. Yes. I 'ad enough a that pair last time.

She steps into one shoe.

We're only goin' for the big film. She can do what she likes outside.

LEN (*gives her the other shoe*). Thass yer lot.

MARY. 'E wants lockin' up for life. Ta, dear. I don't expect yer t' understand at your age, but things don't turn out too bad. There's always someone worse off in the world.

LEN (*clearing up the polishing things*). Yer can always be that one.

MARY. She's my own flesh an' blood, but she don't take after me. Not a thought in 'er 'ead. She's 'ad a rough time a it. I feel sorry for 'er about the kid –

LEN. One a them things. Yer can't make too much a it.

MARY. Never 'ave 'appened if she'd a look after it right. Yer done a lovely job on these. What yer doin' t'night?

LEN (*sews a button on his shirt*). Gettin' ready for work.

MARY. Yer don't go out so much.

LEN. I was out Tuesday.

MARY. Yer ought a be out every night.

LEN. Can't afford it.

MARY. There's plenty a nice girls round 'ere.

LEN. I ain' got the energy these days. They want – somethin' flash.

MARY. Yer can't tell me what they want. I was the same that age.

LEN. I ain' got time for 'alf a 'em. They don't know what they got it for.

MARY. I thought that's what you men were after.

LEN. 'Alf a 'em, it ain' worth the bother a gettin' there. Thass a fact.

MARY. What about the other 'alf?

LEN. Hm!

MARY (*having trouble with her suspender*). Yer 'ave t' go about it the right way. Yer can't stand a girl in a puddle down the back a some ol' alley an' think yer doin' 'er a favour. Yer got yer own room upstairs. That's a nice room. Surprised yer don't use that. I don't mind what goes on, yer know that. As long as yer keep the noise down.

LEN. Ta.

MARY. It's in every man. It 'as t' come out.

Pause.

We didn't carry on like that when I was your age.

LEN. Pull the other one.

MARY. Not till yer was in church. Anyway, yer 'ad t' be engaged. I think it's nicer in the open. I do.

LEN. I bet yer bin up a few alleys.

MARY. You enjoy yerself. I know what I'd be doin' if I was you.

LEN. You meetin' a fella?

MARY. No! I'm goin' out with Mrs Lee.

LEN. Waste.

MARY. Don't be cheeky.

LEN. Yer look fair when yer all done up.

MARY. What you after? Bin spendin' me rent money?

LEN. Wass on?

MARY. Don't know. Somethin' daft.

LEN. Shall I look it up?

MARY. They're all the same. Sex. Girls 'angin' out a their dresses an' men bendin' over 'em.

LEN. It's one of them nudes. 'Eard the fellas talkin'.

MARY. Shan't go in.

LEN. Don't know what yer missin'.

MARY. Different for men.

LEN. Always full a tarts when I bin.

MARY. Thass where yer spend yer money.

LEN. Very nice. Big ol' tits bouncin' about in sinner-scope.

MARY. Don't think Mrs Lee'd fancy that.

LEN. I'll 'ave t' take yer one a these nights.

MARY. I'd rather see Tarzan.

LEN. Thass easy, come up next time I 'ave a bath.

MARY. Count the 'airs on yer chest?

LEN. For a start.

MARY. Sounds like a 'orror film.

LEN. I enjoy a good scrub. On me back.

MARY. Thass the regular carry-on in China.

LEN. No 'arm in it.

MARY. No.

Slight pause.

Pam's very easy goin' for a nice girl. I suppose yer miss that.

LEN. Takes a bit a gettin' used to.

MARY. 'Ow'd yer manage?

LEN. Any suggestions?

Slight pause.

MARY. Bugger!

LEN. Eh?

MARY. Thass tore it!

LEN. Wass up?

MARY. O blast! I caught me stockin'.

LEN. O.

MARY. That would 'ave to 'appen.

LEN. 'Ow'd yer do it?

MARY. Juss when I'm late. Bugger it.

She looks in the table drawer.

'Ardly worth goin' in a minute. Excuse my language. Never find anythin' when yer want it in this place.

LEN. What yer lost?

MARY. It's the only decent pair I got.

LEN. Thass a shame.

MARY. It'll run.

LEN. Less 'ave a shufties.

MARY. Caught on that blasted chair. It's bin like that for ages.

LEN. Yeh. Thass a big one.

MARY. Pam's got 'er nail-varnish all over the place except when yer wan'a find it.

LEN (*offers her the needle*). 'Ave a loan of this.

MARY. It'll run, y'see.

LEN. Less do the cotton.

MARY. I certainly can't afford new ones this week.

LEN (*threading the needle*). Not t' worry.

MARY. I'm no good at that.

LEN. Well, 'ave a bash.

MARY. It'll make it worse.

LEN. No it won't.

MARY (*puts her foot on the chair seat*). You do it.

LEN. Me?

MARY. I never could use a needle. I should a bin there by now.

LEN. I don't know if I –

MARY. Get on. It's only doin' me a good turn.

LEN. It ain' that. I –

MARY. Mrs Lee's waitin'. I can't take 'em off. I'm in ever such a 'urry. They'll run.

LEN. Yeh. It's dodgy. I don't wan'a prick –

MARY. Yer got steady 'ands your age.

LEN (*kneels in front of her and starts darning*). Yeh. (*He drops the needle*). O.

MARY. All right?

LEN. It's dropped.

MARY. What?

LEN. Me needle.

MARY. Yer're 'oldin' me up.

LEN (*on his hands and knees*). 'Ang on.

MARY. That it?

LEN. No.

MARY (*she helps him to look*). Can't a got far.

LEN. It's gone.

MARY. What's that?

LEN. Where?

MARY. That's it. There.

LEN. O. Ta.

MARY (*puts her foot back on the chair*). I ain' got all night.

LEN. I'll 'ave t' get me 'and inside.

MARY. You watch where yer go. Yer ain' on yer 'oneymoon yet. Yer 'and's cold!

LEN. Keep still, or it'll jab yer.

MARY. You watch yerself.

LEN. I'll juss give it a little stretch.

MARY. All right?

LEN. Yer got lovely legs.

MARY. You get on with it.

LEN. Lovely an' smooth.

MARY. Never mind my legs.

LEN. It's a fact.

MARY. Some people'd 'ave a fit if they 'eard that. Yer know what they're like.

LEN. Frustrated.

MARY. I'm old enough t' be yer mother.

HARRY *comes in. He goes straight to the table.*

To LEN. Go steady!

LEN. Sorry.

MARY. You watch where yer pokin'. That 'urt.

LEN. I tol' yer t' keep still.
MARY. Yer'll make it bigger, not smaller.

HARRY *takes ink and a Pools coupon from the table drawer.*
He puts them on the table.

LEN. That'll see yer through t'night.

He ties a knot in the thread.

MARY. Wass up now?
LEN. Scissors.
MARY. Eh?
LEN. I 'ad 'em juss now.
MARY. Bite it.
LEN. Eh?
MARY. Go on.
LEN (*leans forward*). Keep still.
MARY. I can't wait all night.

LEN *bites the thread off.* HARRY *goes out.*

  Took yer time.
LEN (*stands*). Ow! I'm stiff.
MARY (*looks*). Ta, very nice.
LEN. Ain' worth goin' now.
MARY. 'Ave I got me cigarettes?
LEN. Might be somethin' on telly.
MARY. I can't disappoint Mrs Lee.
LEN. I 'ad a feelin' 'e'd come in.
MARY. Yer'll be in bed time I get back.
LEN. She won't wait this long.
MARY. I'll say good night. Thanks for 'elpin'.
LEN. Stay in an' put yer feet up. I'll make us a cup of tea.
MARY. Can't let yer friends down. Cheerio.
LEN. Okay.

MARY *goes.* LEN *takes a handkerchief from his pocket. He*
switches the light off and goes to the couch.

SCENE TEN

A café.

  Furniture: chairs and three tables, one up right, one right and one down left. Apart from this the stage is bare.

LEN *and* PAM *sit at the table up right.*

LEN (*drinks tea*). Warms yer up.

Pause.

  These early mornin's knock me out. 'Nother cup?

Pause.

PAM. Wass the time?
LEN. Quarter past.
PAM. Why ain't they got a clock?

Pause.

LEN. 'Ave another one.
PAM. Thass the fourth time yer keep arstin.
LEN. Warm yer up.
PAM. Go an' sit on yer own table.

Pause.

LEN. Sure yer wrote the name right?
PAM. We'll look bloody daft when 'e finds you 'ere. Wass 'e goin' to say?
LEN. 'Ello.

Pause.

  Let me go an' find 'im.
PAM. No.
LEN. There's no use –

PAM. No!

LEN. Suit yerself.

PAM. Do I 'ave t' say everythin' twice?

LEN. There's no need t' shout.

PAM. I ain' shoutin'.

LEN. They can 'ear yer 'alf way t' –

PAM. I don't wan'a know.

LEN. Yer never do.

Silence.

PAM. Len. I don't want a keep on at yer. I don't know what's
the matter with me. They wan'a put the 'eat on. It's like
death. Yer'd get on a lot better with someone else.

LEN. Per'aps 'e ain' comin'.

PAM. They must 'ave all the winders open. It's no life for
a fella. Yer ain' a bad sort.

LEN. Yeh. I'm goin' a be late in.

PAM. Don't go.

LEN. You make me money up?

PAM *(after a slight pause).* Why can't yer go somewhere?

LEN. Where?

PAM. There's lots a places.

LEN. 'Easy t' say.

PAM. I'll find yer somewhere.

LEN. I ain' scuttlin' off juss t' make room for you t' shag in.

PAM. Yer're a stubborn sod! Don't blame me what 'appens
t' yer! Yer ain' messin' me about again.

LEN. I knew that wouldn't last long!

PAM. I'm sick t' death a yer. Clear off!

She goes to the table down left and sits. LEN *goes out left. Pause.
He comes back with a cup of tea. He puts it on the table in front of*
PAM. *He stands near the table.*

LEN. It'll get cold.

Pause.

Did 'e say 'e'd come?

Pause.

Did 'e answer any a your letters?

She re-acts.

I juss wondered!
PAM. I tol' yer before!
LEN. Thass all right then.

Pause.

PAM. It's like winter in 'ere.

There are voices off right. Someone shouts. A door bangs open.
MIKE, COLIN, PETE, BARRY, FRED *and* LIZ *come in.*

COLIN. 'Ere we are again.
BARRY. Wipe yer boots.
MIKE. On you!
BARRY. Where we sittin'?
MIKE. On yer 'ead.
BARRY. On me arse!
LIZ. Don't know 'ow 'e tells the difference.

She laughs.

FRED. This'll do.
PETE. All right?
LIZ. Can I sit 'ere?
MIKE. Sit where yer like, dear.
BARRY. What we 'avin'?
PETE (*to* FRED). What yer fancy?
FRED. What they got?
PETE (*looks left*). Double egg, bacon, 'am, bangers, double
    bangers, sper-gety –
BARRY. Chips.
FRED. Juss bring the lot.

PETE. Oi, ease off.

FRED. An' four cups a tea.

PETE. I'm standin' yer for this!

FRED. Make that twice.

BARRY. An' me!

PETE (*to* LIZ). Wass yourn, darlin'?

FRED. Now or later?

PETE. Now, t' start with.

BARRY. Tea and crumpet.

LIZ. Could I 'ave a coffee?

FRED. 'Ave what yer like, darlin'.

BARRY. Cup a tea do me!

COLIN. Wass she 'avin' later!

LIZ. Dinner.

MIKE. Teas all round then.

BARRY. Right.

MIKE (*to* FRED). Sit down, we'll fix it.

PETE, MIKE *and* COLIN *go off left.*

FRED. Where's all the burn?

LIZ. I only got one left.

FRED (*calls*). Get us some snout.

MIKE. Five or ten?

FRED *makes a rude gesture.* LIZ *offers him her cigarette.*

FRED. Keep it, darlin'. I'm okay.
He turns to LEN *and* PAM. Oi, 'ello then. 'Ow's it goin'?

He stands and goes down to their table. LEN *has already sat.*

PAM. 'Ello.

FRED. Thass right, yer said yer'd be 'ere. (*Calls.*) That grub
ready? (*To* PAM.) Yeh.

BARRY (*to* FRED). Big gut!

COLIN (*off*). Give us a chance!

PETE (*off*). They didn't teach yer no manners inside.

FRED. Yer're arstin' for trouble. I don't wan'a go back juss yet.

PAM. You all right?

FRED. Yeh. You look all right.

LIZ. Don't yer reckon 'e looks thin?

PAM. I can't –

LIZ. Like a rake. I tol' yer, didn't I? Yer wan'a get some meat on yer.

FRED. I will when that grub turns up.

BARRY *and* LIZ *are sitting at the table up right.* BARRY *bangs the table.*

BARRY. Grub!

COLIN (*off*). Ease up, louse!

BARRY (*calls*). Make that two coffees. (*He puts on an accent.*) I feel like a cup.

LIZ. Ain' what yer sound like.

PETE (*off*). Shut 'im up!

BARRY *makes a gesture.*

FRED. Why did the policewoman marry the 'angman?

LIZ. Eh?

FRED. They both liked necking.

They laugh.

PETE (*off*). Why was the undertaker buried alive?

LIZ. 'Is job got on top a 'im.

They laugh.

BARRY. Why did the woman with three tits 'ave quads?

MIKE. We 'eard it!

The rest groan.

COLIN (*off*). What about the sailor 'oo drowned in 'is bath?

FRED. 'Is brother was the fireman 'oo went up in smoke.

They laugh.

PETE (*off*). Didn't know they let yer 'ave jokes inside.

LIZ. Wass it like?

FRED. In there?

LIZ. Yeh.

FRED (*shrugs. To* LEN). 'Ow's the job?

LEN. Stinks.

FRED. It don't change. (*He sits at their table.*) Long time.

LIZ. Got a light?

FRED (*to* PAM). I got yer letters didn't I.

PAM. Yeh.

FRED. I ain' good at writin'.

PETE, COLIN *and* MIKE *shout and laugh, off.*

PAM. Where yer goin'?

FRED. I'm goin' to 'ave the biggest nosh-up a me life.

BARRY (*to* FRED). Did yer be'ave yerself inside?

PAM (*to* FRED). No, after that.

FRED. O yer know.

PAM. Yer fixed up?

FRED. 'Ow?

PAM. I'll take yer roun' our place.

FRED. O –

LEN. Yer can muck in with me a couple a nights. Give yerself
    time t' get straight.

FRED. Ta, I don't wan' a put –

LEN. Yer won't be in the way for a couple of days.

PAM. Mum'll shut up. It'll be nice and quiet. Thass what
    yer need.

FRED. Yer must be kidding!

BARRY (*to* LIZ). Arst 'im if 'e be'aved isself.

LIZ (*to* FRED). 'Ear that?

FRED. Yer know me.

BARRY. Not 'arf.

FRED. One day.

LIZ. Yeh.

FRED. This padre 'as me in.

BARRY. O yeh.

FRED. Wants t' chat me up. 'E says nothin that comes out a a man can be all bad.

BARRY. Whass that?

FRED. Then 'e 'ops out an' I 'as a little slash in 'is tea.

LIZ *and* BARRY *laugh* – LIZ *very loudly.*

LIZ. What 'appened?

FRED. 'E reckoned they ain' put the sugar in.

They laugh.

Another bloke –

LIZ. Yeh.

FRED. Stares at me. Keeps starin' at me. All day. It's 'is first day, see.

BARRY. Go on.

FRED. So I gets 'im on the landin' an' clobbers 'im.

BARRY. Bang!

FRED. An' it only turns out 'e'd got a squint!

They laugh.

LIZ. Wass it like inside?

FRED. I got chokey for the clobberin'. Bread and water!

BARRY. On yer jack.

FRED. Only good thing there's no one t' scrounge yer grub.

BARRY. Yer d'narf tell 'em.

FRED. Ain' my sort a life. Glad I done it once, but thass their lot. Ain' pinnin' nothin' on me next time.

LIZ. Wass it like?

FRED. In there?

LIZ. Yeh.

FRED. Cold.

LIZ. Eh?

FRED. Cold.

Silence. MIKE *comes in a few paces from the left.*

MIKE. Won't be 'alf a jik.

FRED. 'Bout time.

COLIN (*off*). 'E still moanin'?

COLIN *comes on and stands with* MIKE.

FRED. Eh?

COLIN. Bet yer couldn't carry-on in there.

FRED. Lot I couldn't do in there, if yer like t' look at it.

MIKE. We ain' got a treat yer everyday.

FRED. I'll pay for this if you like. (*To* LIZ.) Lend us ten bob.

PETE *comes in.*

PETE. 'Oo arst yer t' pay?

FRED. I reckon it's worth one lousy meal.

PETE. Yer made yer own decisions, didn't yer?

BARRY (*comes down*). Wass up?

PETE. We ain' got a crawl up yer arse.

COLIN. Grub smell all right, don't –

PETE. 'Ang on a minute, Col.

MIKE (*to* PETE). Nah, it's 'is first day out, Pete. Let 'im settle down.

COLIN. Come on.

He starts to go left.

PETE. 'E ain' swingin' that one on me.

PETE *and* COLIN *go out left.*

MIKE (*to* FRED). 'E got out the wrong bed this mornin'.

MIKE *follows them off. Slight pause.*

FRED (*laughs*). It's the ol' lag comin' out a me! (*Shouts.*) Whoopee!

BARRY. Ha-ha! Whoopee!

FRED.

      She was only a goalkeeper's daughter
      She married a player called Jack

        It was great when 'e played centre forward
        But 'e liked to slip round to the back.
  (*He laughs.*) I used a lie in me pit thinkin' a that.

COLIN (*off*): What?

FRED: Nosh.

LIZ. That all?

FRED. An' tryin' a remember whass up your legs.

LIZ. I'll draw yer a picture. Give us a light.

FRED (*to* PAM). Give 'er a light.

He gives her a box of matches. She takes them to LIZ. *To*
LEN. Wass 'er game?

LEN. I don't wan'a get involved, mate.

FRED. Yeh? Yer should a read them crummy letters she
  keeps sendin'. She ain' goin' a catch me round 'er place.

LEN. No. What was it like?

FRED. No, talk about somethin' else.

LEN. No, *before.*

FRED. Yer 'eard the trial.

PAM *comes back to the table.*

  Go away, Pam.

PAM. I wan' a finish me tea.

LEN. Thass cold.

FRED. Can't yer take a 'int? Take yer tea over there.

PAM. Wass goin' on?

LEN. Nothin'!

FRED. No one's talkin' about you.

PAM (*going to sit down at the table*). I'd rather –

FRED. O Pam!

She goes to the unoccupied table and watches them.

  'Er ol' people still alive? If yer can call it that.

LEN. Yeh.

FRED. Yer ain' still livin' there?

LEN. I'm goin' soon.

FRED. Yer're as bad as them. She won't get me there in a
   month a Sundays.
LEN. What was it like?
FRED. I tol' yer.
LEN. No, before.
FRED. Before what?
LEN. In the park.
FRED. Yer saw.
LEN. Wass it feel like?
FRED. Don't know.
LEN. When yer was killin' it.
FRED. Do what?
LEN. Wass it feel like when yer killed it?
BARRY (*to* LIZ). Fancy a record?
LIZ. Wouldn't mind.
BARRY. Give us a tanner then.
LIZ. Yer're as tight as a flea's arse'ole.
BARRY. An 'alf as 'andsome. I know. – Out a change.

LIZ *gives him sixpence. He goes off down right.* MIKE *brings on
two cups.*

MIKE. Comin' up.
FRED. Very 'andy.
BARRY (*off*). 'Ow about 'I Broke my 'Eart'?
LIZ. Yeh. Thass great.
BARRY (*off*). Well they ain' got it.
LIZ. Funny! What about 'My 'Eart is Broken'?
MIKE (*to* LIZ). One coffee.
BARRY (*off*). They got that.
LIZ (*to* MIKE). The sugar in it?
MIKE. Taste it.

MIKE *goes off left.*

LEN. Whass it like, Fred?
FRED (*drinks*). It ain' like this in there.

LEN. Fred.

FRED. I tol' yer.

LEN. No yer ain'.

FRED. I forget.

LEN. I thought yer'd a bin full a it. I was –

FRED. Len!

LEN. – curious, thass all, 'ow it feels t' –

FRED. No!

He slams his fist on the table.

LEN. Okay.

FRED. It's finished.

LEN. Yeh.

FRED (*stands*). What yer wan' a do?

The juke box starts.

LEN. Nothin'.

FRED. Wass 'e gettin' at?

LEN. It's finished.

PETE, MIKE, COLIN *and* BARRY *come on.* PAM *stands.* LIZ
still sits.

FRED. I were'n the only one.

LEN. I ain' gettin' at yer, skip.

PETE. Wass up?

FRED. Nothin' a do with you.

PAM. 'E was rowin'.

FRED. It's nothin'. Where's that grub?

PAM. I knew 'e'd start somethin'.

FRED. Forget it.

PAM. I tol' 'im not t' come.

FRED. Where's that flippin' grub? Move.

COLIN *and* MIKE *go off left.*

PAM. 'E won't let me alone.

FRED. I'm starvin' I know that.

PAM. 'E follers me everywhere.

FRED. Ain' you lucky.

PAM. Tell 'im for me! 'It 'im! 'It 'im!

FRED. It's nothin' a do with me!

PAM. It is! It is!

BARRY. She's started.

FRED. 'Ere we go!

He sits and puts his head in his hands.

PAM (*to* LEN). See what yer done?

FRED. Didn't take 'er long.

PAM. It's your place t' stick up for me, love. I went through all that trouble for you! Somebody's got a save me from 'im.

FRED. Thanks. Thanks very much. I'll remember this.

He stands and starts back to his own table.

LIZ (*starting to click her fingers*). I can't 'ear the music!

PAM (*to* LEN). Don't bloody sit there! Yer done enough 'arm!

PETE 'Oo brought 'er 'ere?

FRED. Chriss knows!

PAM (*pointing to* LEN). 'E started this!

FRED. I don't care what bleedin' wet started it. You can stop it!

PAM (*to* LEN). I 'ate yer for this!

FRED. BELT UP!

PAM (*goes to* FRED, *who sits at his table*). I'm sorry. Fred, 'e's goin' now. It'll be all right when 'e's gone.

LEN *does not move.*

FRED. All right.

PAM (*looks round*). Where's 'is grub? 'E's starvin' 'ere. (*She goes to touch his arm.*) I get so worked up when 'e –

FRED. Keep yer 'ands off me! So 'elp me I'll land yer so bloody 'ard they'll put me back for life!

PETE (*moving in*). Right. Less get ourselves sorted out.

COLIN *comes on left.*

PAM. It don't matter. I juss got excited. (*Calls.*) Where's 'is
breakfast? It'll be time for –

FRED. Breakfast? I couldn't eat in this bloody place if they
served it through a rubber tube.

PETE. Come on! (*Calls.*) Mike!

FRED. All I done for 'er an' she 'as the bloody nerve t' start
this!

PETE. Come on, less move.

BARRY. She wants throttlin'.

MIKE *comes on left.* COLIN *and* FRED *go out right. The door*
bangs.

LIZ. I ain' drunk me coffee.

PETE. I said move!

MIKE. Flippin' mad'ouse.

MIKE *goes out right. The door bangs.*

LIZ. We paid for it!

PETE. Move!

LIZ *and* BARRY *go out right. The door bangs.*

You come near 'im again an' I'll settle yer for good.
Lay off.

PETE *goes out right. The door bangs.* LEN *still sits.* PAM *stands.*
Pause.

LEN. I'll see yer 'ome. I'm late for work already. I know I'm
in the way. Yer can't go round the streets when yer're like
that. (*He hesitates.*) They ain' done 'im no good. 'Es gone
back like a kid. Yer well out a it. (*He stands.*) I knew the
little bleeder 'ld do a bunk! Can't we try an' get on like
before? (*He looks round.*) There's no one else. Yer only
live once.

SCENE ELEVEN

The living-room.

On the table: bread, butter, breadknife, cup and saucer and milk.

MARY sits on the couch.

HARRY comes in with a pot of tea. He goes to the table. He cuts and butters bread. Pause while he works.

MARY goes out. HARRY goes on working. MARY comes back with a cup and saucer. She pours herself tea. She takes it to the couch and sits. She sips.

HARRY moves so that his back is to her. He puts his cup upright in his saucer. He puts milk in the cup. He reaches to pick up the teapot.

MARY stands, goes to the table, and moves the teapot out of his reach. She goes back to the couch. Sits. Sips.

MARY. My teapot.

Sips. Pause.

HARRY. My tea.

He pours tea into his cup. MARY stands and goes to the table. She empties his cup on the floor.

HARRY. Our'n. Weddin' present.
MARY (*goes to the couch and sits*). From *my* mother.
HARRY. That was joint.
MARY. Don't you dare talk to me!

HARRY goes out.

MARY (*loudly*). Some minds want boilin' in carbolic. Soap's too good for 'em. (*Slight pause.*) Dirty filth! Worse! Ha! (*She goes to the door and calls*). Don't you dare talk to me!

She goes to the couch and sits. HARRY comes in.

HARRY. I'll juss say one word. I saw yer with yer skirt up.
Yer call me filth?

*HARRY goes out. Slight pause. MARY goes to the table and
empties his slices of bread on to the floor. She goes back to the
couch and drinks her tea.*

MARY. Mind out of a drain! I wouldn't let a kid like that touch
me if 'e paid for it!

HARRY comes in. He goes straight to the table.

HARRY. I don't want to listen.
MARY. Filth!
HARRY. There's bin enough trouble in this 'ouse. Now yer
wan'a cause trouble with 'im!
MARY. Don't talk t' me! You!
HARRY (*sees his bread on the floor*). Yer juss wan'a start trouble
like there was before! (*He stoops and picks up the bread.*)
Middle-age woman – goin' with 'er own daughter's left-
overs – 'alf 'er age – makin' 'erself a spectacle – look at this!
– No self control.
MARY. Filth!
HARRY. Like a child – I pity the lad – must want 'is 'ead
tested.
MARY. There'll be some changes in this 'ouse. I ain' puttin'
up with this after t'day. Yer can leave my things alone for
a start. All this stuff come out a my pocket. I worked for it!
I ain' 'avin' you dirtyin' me kitchin. Yer can get yerself
some new towels for a start! An' plates! An' knives! An'
cups! Yer'll soon find a difference!
HARRY. Don't threaten me –
MARY. An' my cooker! An' my curtains! An' my sheets!
HARRY. Yer'll say somethin' yer'll be sorry for!

*He comes towards her. There is a chair in the way. He trips over
it. The leg comes off.*

MARY. Don't you touch me!

HARRY. Two can play at your game! Yeh! I can stop your money t'morra!

MARY. Don't yer raise yer 'and t' me!

HARRY *goes back to the table. He starts cutting bread. Pause.*

I knew yer was stood outside when 'e was there. I 'eard yer through the door. I'd a bet my life you'd come in!

HARRY. Old enough t' be 'is mother. Yer must be 'ard up!

MARY. I seen you stuck 'ere long enough! You couldn't pick an' choose!

HARRY. One was enough.

MARY. No one else would a put up with yer!

HARRY. I can do without! Yer ain' worth it!

MARY. Ha! I saw yer face when yer come through that door. I bin watchin' yer all the week. I know you of old, Harry!

HARRY. Yer'll go out a yer mind one day!

MARY. Filth!

HARRY. I 'ad enough a you in the past! I ain' puttin' up with your lark again. I'm too old. I wan' a bit a peace an' quiet.

MARY. Then why did yer come in?

HARRY. Me pools was in that table.

MARY. Yer was spyin'! Yer bin sniffin' round ever since! I ain' puttin' up with your dirt! (*She picks up the teapot.*) Yer can bloody well stay in yer room!

PAM *comes in.*

PAM. Chriss. (*Calls.*) It's them!

HARRY (*cutting bread*). I ain' sunk so low I'll bother *you*!

MARY. Yer jealous ol' swine!

HARRY. Of a bag like you?

MARY. 'E don't think so! I could a gone t'bed, an' I will next time 'e arsts me!

HARRY. Now 'e's caught a sniff a yer 'e'll be off with 'is tail between 'is legs?

She hits him with the teapot. The water pours over him. PAM *is too frightened to move.*

  Ah!

MARY. 'Ope yer die!

HARRY. Blood!

MARY. Use words t' me!

HARRY. Blood!

PAM. Mum!

HARRY. Ah!

LEN (*off*). Whass up?

HARRY. Doctor.

MARY. Cracked me weddin' present. 'Im.

LEN *comes in.*

LEN. Blimey!

HARRY. Scalded!

PAM. Whass 'appenin'?

HARRY. She tried t' murder me!

MARY. Yer little liar!

PAM. Are yer all right?

HARRY. Yer saw 'er.

MARY. 'E went mad.

LEN. It's only a scratch.

PAM (*to* MARY). Why?

MARY. 'Effin an' blindin'.

LEN. Yer'll live.

HARRY. Blood.

PAM (*to* MARY). Whass 'e done?

LEN. 'E's all wet.

MARY. Swore at me!

PAM. Why?

HARRY. Doctor.

MARY. There's nothin' wrong with 'im.

HARRY. Scalded.

MARY. I 'ardly touched 'im. 'E needs a good thrashin'!

LEN (*to* PAM). Get a towel.

HARRY. I ain' allowed t' touch the towels.

MARY. I kep' this twenty-three years. Look what 'e's done to it!

PAM. *What 'appened?*

LEN. Nothin'. They 'ad a row.

PAM. 'E called 'er a bag.

LEN. It's nothin'. I'd better be off t' work. They'll give us me cards. We juss seen Fred. 'E looks all right, well 'e don't look bad. It ain' Butlins. (*To* PAM.) Get 'im up t' bed. Put the kettle on. Yer could all do with a cup a tea.

PAM (*to* MARY). What made yer start talkin'?

MARY. Yer 'eard 'im call me a bag. (*To* LEN.) 'E went mad over catchin' you last week.

LEN (*looking at* HARRY's *head*). Yer'll 'ave t' wash that cut. It's got tealeaves in it.

HARRY *dabs at it with the tail of his shirt.*

PAM. Caught 'oo last week?

MARY (*pointing to* HARRY). 'Is filth. (*Points to* LEN.) Arst 'im!

PAM (*to* LEN). What 'appened?

LEN. Nothin'.

HARRY. I was cuttin' bread. (*He picks up the knife.*) She flew at me!

PAM (*to* LEN). I knew it was you! (*To* HARRY.) Whass 'e done?

LEN. Nothin'.

MARY. Filth!

HARRY. I found 'em both.

He points with the knife to the spot.

LEN (*pulling at* HARRY). No!

HARRY. She'll 'ave t' 'ear.

LEN (*he pulls at him*). No!

HARRY. She 'ad 'er clothes up.

PAM. No!

LEN. Yer bloody fool! Yer bloody, bloody fool!

LEN *shakes* HARRY. *The knife waves through the air.*

HARRY. Ah!

PAM. That knife!

MARY. Filth!

PAM. 'E'll kill 'im!

LEN. Bloody fool.

PAM (*screams*). Oh! No! – Whass 'appenin' to us?

She sits on the couch and cries. Pause.

HARRY. 'Im an' 'er.

PAM (*crying*). Why don't 'e go? Why don't 'e go away?
All my friends gone. Baby's gone. Nothin' left but rows.
Day in, day out. Fightin' with knives.

HARRY. I'm shakin'.

PAM (*crying*). They'll kill each other soon.

LEN (*to* PAM). Yer can't blame them on me!

PAM (*crying*). Why can't 'e go away!

HARRY (*removes his shirt*). Wet.

PAM (*crying*). Look at me. I can't sleep with worry.

MARY. Breakin' me 'ome.

PAM (*crying*). 'E's killed me baby. Taken me friends. Broken
me 'ome.

HARRY. More blood.

MARY. I ain' clearin' up after 'im. 'E can clear 'is own mess.

PAM (*crying*). I can't go on like this.

LEN (*to* PAM). There was nothin' in it!

PAM (*crying*). I'll throw myself somewhere. It's the only way.

HARRY. Cold.

LEN *goes to* HARRY.

PAM (*sitting and crying*). Stop 'im! They'll kill each other!

LEN (*stops*). I was goin' a 'elp 'im.

PAM (*crying*). Take that knife. The baby's dead. They're all
gone. It's the only way. I can't go on.

MARY. Next time 'e won't be so lucky.

PAM (*crying*). Yer can't call it livin'. 'E's pullin' me t' pieces. Nothin' but trouble.

LEN. I'm tryin' t' 'elp! 'Oo else'll 'elp? If I go will they come back? Will the baby come back? Will 'e come back? I'm the only one that's stayed an' yer wan'a get rid a me!

PAM (*crying*). I can't stand any more. Baby dead. No friends.

LEN. I'll go.

PAM (*crying*). No one listens. Why don't 'e go? Why don't they make 'im go?

MARY. 'E can stay in 'is own room after t'day.

LEN. I'll find somewhere dinnertime.

HARRY. Me neck's throbbin'.

PAM (*crying*). No 'ome. No friends. Baby dead. Gone. Fred gone.

SCENE TWELVE

LEN's *bedroom.*

LEN *lies face down on the floor. The side of his face is flat against the floorboards. He holds a knife. There is an open suitcase on the bed. In it are a few things. Pause.*

The door opens. HARRY *comes in. He wears long white combinations. He wears pale socks. No shoes. His head is in a skull cap of bandages. He comes up behind* LEN. LEN *sees him slowly.*

HARRY. Evenin'.

LEN. Evenin'.

HARRY. Get up. Yer'll catch cold down there.

LEN. 'Ow's yer 'ead?

HARRY (*touches it*). Don't know.

LEN. Thass a good sign.

HARRY. All right now?

LEN. I was listenin'.

He draws the knife between two boards.

Clears the crack. Yer can 'ear better.

HARRY. Thass a good knife.

LEN. She's got someone with 'er.

HARRY. Thought yer might like someone t' say good night.

LEN. Yer can 'ear 'er voice.

HARRY. No.

LEN. She's picked someone up. I couldn't get anywhere with me packin'.

HARRY. No, I saw 'er come in.

LEN. Could a swore I 'eard someone.

HARRY. Not with 'er!

LEN. She's still good lookin'.

HARRY. 'Er sort's two a penny. Lads don't 'ave t' put up with 'er carry-on.

LEN. I used t' 'ear Fred an' her down there.

HARRY. No more.

LEN. Kep' me awake.

HARRY (*sits on the bed*). Tired. Nice 'ere.

LEN. Seen worse.

HARRY. Quiet.

LEN. Sometimes.

Pause.

HARRY. She's cryin'.

LEN. O.

HARRY. In bed. I passed 'er door.

LEN. I knew I 'eard somethin'.

HARRY. Thass what yer 'eard.

LEN *puts a pair of socks in the case.*

Won't be the last time.

LEN. Eh?

HARRY. 'Owlin in bed.

LEN. O.

HARRY. She'll pay for it.
LEN. What?
HARRY. 'Er ways. Yer'll get yer own back.
LEN. I lost me case keys.
HARRY. Yer'll see.
LEN. Long time since I used it.
HARRY. Where yer goin'?
LEN. 'Ad enough.
HARRY. No different any other place.
LEN. I've heard it all before.

Pause.

HARRY. Thought yer'd like t' say good night.
LEN. Yeh. Ta.
HARRY. They're all in bed.
LEN. I get in the way, don't I?
HARRY. Take no notice.
LEN. Sick a rows.
HARRY. They've 'ad their say. They'll keep quiet now.
LEN. I upset every –
HARRY. No different if yer go. They won't let yer drop.
LEN. Different for me.

He puts a shirt in the case.

I never put a finger on your ol' woman. I juss give 'er a 'and.
HARRY. I known 'er longer'n you.
LEN. She reckoned she was late.
HARRY. Ain' my worry.
LEN. But yer 'ad a row.
HARRY. She 'ad a row.
LEN. You shouted.
HARRY. It ain' like that.
LEN. I 'eard yer.
HARRY. It clears the air. Sometimes. It's finished. – You
shouted.

Pause.

LEN. I'll 'ave t' look for that key.

HARRY. I left 'er once.

LEN. You?

HARRY. I come back.

LEN. Why?

HARRY. I worked it out. Why should I soil me 'ands washin' an' cookin'? Let 'er do it. She'll find out.

LEN. Yer do yer own washin'.

HARRY. Eh?

LEN. An' cookin'.

HARRY. Ah, *now.*

Pause.

LEN. I can do without the key. I ain' goin' far.

HARRY. Bin in the army?

LEN. No.

HARRY. Yer can see that. Know where yer goin'?

LEN. Someplace 'andy. For work.

HARRY. Round Fred?

LEN. No.

HARRY. She won't see 'im again.

LEN. Best thing, too. Yer ain' seen what it done t' 'im. 'E's like a kid. 'E'll finished up like some ol' lag, or an' ol' soak. Bound to. An' soon. Yer'll see.

He moves the case along the bed.

That'll keep till t'morrow.

HARRY. It's a shame.

LEN. Too tired t'night. Wass a shame?

HARRY. Yer stood all the rows. Now it'll settle down an' yer –

LEN. I 'ad my last row, I know that.

HARRY. Sit 'ere.

LEN (*sits on the bed*). It's bin a 'ard day.

HARRY. Finished now.

A long pause.

LEN. I'd like t' get up t'morrow mornin' and clear right out. There's nothin' t' keep me 'ere. What do I get out a it? Jack it in. Emigrate.

HARRY. Yer're too young t' emigrate. Do that when yer past fifty.

LEN. I don't give a damn if they don't talk, but they don't even listen t' yer. Why the 'ell should I bother about 'er?

HARRY. It's juss a rough patch. We 'ad t' sort ourselves out when you joined us. But yer fit in now. It'll settle down.

LEN. No one tells yer anything really.

Slight pause.

Was she all right?

HARRY. Eh?

LEN. In bed.

HARRY. Yer know.

LEN. No.

HARRY. Up t' the man.

LEN. Yeh?

HARRY. I 'ad the best.

LEN. Go on.

HARRY (*quietly*). I 'ad 'er squealing like a pig.

LEN. Yeh.

HARRY. There was a little boy first.

LEN. In the war.

HARRY. Then the girl.

LEN. On leave.

HARRY. An' back t' the front.

LEN. Go on.

HARRY. I saw the lot.

LEN. What was it like?

HARRY. War?

Slight pause.

Most I remember the peace an' quiet. Once or twice the
'ole lot blew up. Not more. Then it went quiet. Everythin'
still. Yer don't get it that quiet now.

LEN. Not 'ere.

HARRY. Nowhere.

LEN. Kill anyone?

HARRY. Must 'ave. Yer never saw the bleeders, 'ceptin'
prisoners or dead. Well, I did once. I was in a room. Some
bloke stood up in the door. Lost, I expect. I shot 'im. 'E
fell down. Like a coat fallin' off a 'anger, I always say. Not
a word.

Pause.

Yer never killed yer man. Yer missed that. Gives yer a sense
a perspective. I was one a the lucky ones.

Pause.

LEN. 'Oo tied your 'ead?

HARRY. I managed. I never arst them.

LEN. I'm good at that.

HARRY. No need.

Pause.

Nigh on midnight.

LEN. Gone.

He takes off his shoes and stands. He drops his trousers.

HARRY. Yer don't wan'a go.

LEN. Eh?

HARRY. Don't go. No point.

LEN (*his trousers round his ankles*). Why?

HARRY. Yer'd come back.

LEN. No use sayin' anythin' t'night –

HARRY. Don't let 'em push yer out.

LEN. Depends 'ow I feel in the mornin'.

He sits on the bed and pulls off his trousers.

HARRY. Choose yer own time. Not when it suits them.

LEN. I don't know anythin' t'night.

HARRY. I'd like yer t' stay. If yer can see yer way to.

LEN. Why?

HARRY (*after a slight pause*). I ain' stayin'.

LEN. What?

HARRY. Not always.

LEN. O, yeh.

He puts the case on the floor.

HARRY. Yer'll see. If I was t' go now she'd be laughin'. She'd soon 'ave someone in my bed. She knows 'ow t' be'ave when she likes. An' cook.

LEN. Yeh, yeh.

He slides the case under the bed and sits on the bed.

HARRY. I'll go when I'm ready. When she's on 'er pension. She won't get no one after 'er then. I'll be *out*. Then see 'ow she copes.

LEN. Ain' worth it, pop.

HARRY. It's only right. When someone carries on like 'er, they 'ave t' pay for it. People can't get away with murder. What 'd 'appen then?

LEN. Don't arst me.

HARRY. She thinks she's on top. I'll 'ave t' fall back a bit – buy a few things an' stay in me room more. I can wait.

LEN. 'Ead still 'urt?

HARRY. She'll find out.

LEN. I can let yer 'ave some aspirins.

HARRY. Eh?

LEN. Can yer move up.

Harry stands.

No, I didn't mean that.

HARRY. Yer should be in bed. We don't wan'a waste the light.

LEN. I won't let on what yer said.

HARRY. Eh?

LEN. You leavin'.

HARRY. She knows.

LEN. Yer told 'er?

HARRY. We don't 'ave secrets. They make trouble.

He goes to the door.

Don't speak to 'em at all. It saves a lot a misunderstandin'.

LEN. O.

HARRY. Yer'll be all right in the mornin'.

LEN. No work t'night?

HARRY. Saturday.

LEN. I forgot.

HARRY. Night.

LEN. Funny we never talked before.

HARRY. They listen all the time.

LEN. Will yer come up next Saturday night?

HARRY. No, no. Cause trouble. They won't stand for it.

LEN. I'd like t' tell 'er t' jump off once more.

HARRY. Sometime. Don't upset 'er. It ain' fair. Thass best all round.

LEN (*looks round*). It's like that.

HARRY. Listen!

LEN. What?

HARRY *holds up his hand. Silence.*

Still cryin'?

HARRY. She's gone quiet.

Silence.

There – she's movin'.

Silence.

LEN. She's 'eard us.

HARRY. Best keep away, yer see. Good night.
LEN. But –
HARRY. Sh!

He holds up his hand again. They listen. Silence. Pause.

HARRY. Good night.
LEN. 'Night.

HARRY *goes.*

SCENE THIRTEEN

The living-room.

PAM *sits on the couch. She reads the* Radio Times.

MARY *takes things from the table and goes out. Pause. She comes back. She goes to the table. She collects the plates. She goes out.*

Pause. The door opens. HARRY *comes in. He goes to the table and opens the drawer. He searches in it.*

PAM *turns a page.*

MARY *comes in. She goes to the table and picks up the last things on it. She goes out.*

HARRY's *jacket is draped on the back of the chair by the table. He searches in the pockets.*

PAM *turns a page.*

There is a loud bang (off).

Silence.

HARRY *turns to the table and searches in the drawer.*

MARY *comes in. She wipes the table top with a damp cloth.*

There is a loud bang (off).

MARY *goes out.*

HARRY *takes ink and envelope out of the drawer. He puts them on the table. He sits on the chair. He feels behind him and takes a pen from the inside pocket of his jacket. He starts to fill in his football coupon.*

A short silence.

PAM *quickly turns over two pages.*

Immediately the door opens and LEN *comes in. He carries the chair that* HARRY *tripped over and broke. He takes it down right and sets it on the floor. He crouches. His head is below the level of the seat. He looks under the chair. He turns it upside down. He fiddles with the loose leg.*

MARY *comes in. She straightens the couch. She takes off her apron and folds it neatly. She sits on the couch and pushes the apron down the side of the couch.*

Silence.

Stop.

LEN *turns the chair upright. He still crouches. He rests his left wrist high on the chair back and his right elbow on the chair seat. His right hand hangs in space. His back is to the audience. His head is sunk into his shoulders. He thinks for a moment.*

PAM *stands and goes to the door.*

LEN. Fetch me 'ammer.

PAM *goes out.* HARRY *writes.* MARY *sits.* LEN *presses his hand on the seat and the chair wobbles.* MARY *takes up the* Radio Times *and glances at the back page.* HARRY *takes a small leather folder out of the inside pocket of his jacket. He places the folder on the table.*

PAM *comes in and sits on the couch.*

LEN *turns the chair upside down and looks at it.*

MARY *puts the* Radio Times *back on the couch. She pats the pillow.* PAM *picks up the* Radio Times. *In one connected movement* LEN *turns the chair upright and stands to his full height. He has grasped the seat at diagonally opposite corners, so that the diagonal is parallel with the front of his body. He brings the chair sharply down so that the foot furthest from him strikes the floor first. It makes a loud bang. Still standing upright he turns the chair upside down and looks at the leg. He turns the chair upright and sets it down. He crouches. He places the flat of his palm on the seat. The chair still has a little wobble.*

PAM *folds the* Radio Times *and puts it down.*

HARRY *takes a stamp from the folder.* LEN *sits on the chair and faces front. He puts his head between his knees to peer under the chair.* HARRY *licks the stamp and silently stamps the envelope. He reaches behind him and puts the folder and the spare coupon in the inside pocket of his jacket.*

LEN *gets off the chair and crouches beside it. His back is to the audience. He bends over the chair so that his stomach or chest rests on the seat. He reaches down with his left hand and pulls the loose rear leg up into the socket.*

HARRY *reaches behind him and puts his pen into the breast pocket of his jacket. He puts the ink in the table drawer.*

LEN *slips his left arm round the back of the chair. His chest rests against the side edge of the seat. The fingers of his right hand touch the floor. His head lies sideways on the seat.*

MARY *sits.* PAM *sits.*

HARRY *licks the flap on the envelope and closes it quietly.*

The curtain falls quickly.

Notes

(These notes are intended for use by overseas students as well as by British-born readers.)

page

Scene One

11 *on yer tod*: on your own.

12 *Bligh*: expression of surprise, probably short for blimey, see below.

12 *Yer d'narf fidget*: you don't half fidget.

12 *tart*: here just slang for woman, not necessarily understood as derogatory by the person saying it.

13 *yer don't reckon*: you don't like.

14 *arst*: ask.

15 *Wass 'is caper*: what's his game, what's he up to.

15 *'E ain' bin out the back yet*: to the outside lavatory.

15 *twit*: idiot, daft, silly person.

18 *dolly mixture*: small sweets.

18 *ruckin'*: telling off.

Scene Two

19 *still pecky*: still hungry.

21 *blinkin'*: used to intensify expression, probably shortened form of bloody.

26 *navvy*: labourer, someone who digs, short for navigator, someone who dug canals during the Industrial Revolution.

26 *Captain Blood*: sarcastic reference to Len being a pirate.

26 *Very 'ow's yer father*: very fancy.

27 *'avin a bash*: having sex.

27 *I wouldn't mind a bit a grind for you*: pun on the word 'grind', meaning both work and having sex.

Scene Three

28 *nipper*: young child.

28 *revver*: vehicle accelerator.

28 *doin' a ton*: doing 100 miles per hour.
29 *Shootin' up the yeller-niggers*: reference to being in the army in National Service and probably referring to the Korean War.
29 *pig-sticker*: sword.
29 *'e's got a dose*: of venereal disease.
29 *ol' johnny*: old condom.
30 *knocked it off*: had sex.
30 *bollocks*: mild swear word, meaning men's testes.
32 *drops 'er nipper*: has her baby.
32 *scrag-end*: cheapest cut of meat.
33 *put a sock in it*: shut up, shut your mouth.

Scene Four
36 *pokin' 'oles*: criticising.
36 *black an' white minstrels*: reference to a TV show where white actors blacked their faces and sang to look like stereotypical images of black people.
41 *fags*: cigarettes.

Scene Five
45 *give me the 'ump*: makes me fed up, gets me down.
46 *tickets for Crystal Palace*: tickets to see the local football team.

Scene Six
48 *h.p.*: hire purchase, paid for in instalments.
49 *cop*: take.
50 *labour*: labour exchange, job centre.
50 *snout*: cigarettes.
51 *skip*: short for skipper or captain of a ship, sign of respect in the vernacular.
54 *Up the other end*: up to the other end of town, presumably the West End of London, hence the need for fares.
55 *magnetic cobblers*: joking about the attractive power of his testes.
55 *'airy-ated*: aerated, heated.
58 *Blind*: expression of surprise – shortened form of blimey, originally 'blind me' from 'God blind me' (i.e. if I'm not speaking the truth).
59 *Less shift*: let's shift, move.
61 *case round*: look around.
61 *dog-end*: cigarette end after it has been smoked.

64 *Two's up*: I'll take second turn.
67 *cloutin'*: hitting.
67 *sherker*: someone who avoids his or her share of the work.
67 *gungy*: sticky, messy.
68 *'onk like a yid*: it smells like a Jew.
70 *lug 'ole*: ear.
70 *'ooter*: nose.
70 *slasher*: penis.
70 *buck up*: hurry up.
71 *Guy Fawkes*: reference to figure burned annually on 5 November to celebrate the foiling of the plot to blow up Parliament in 1606. Here it refers to the baby as the guy on a bonfire in the pram.
71 *RSPCA*: Royal Society for the Prevention of Cruelty to Animals. He either means the RSPCC, for Prevention of Cruelty to Children, and gets it wrong or is deliberately being cynical.
72 *hacks*: spits.
72 *muggins*: someone stupid.

Scene Seven
73 *Gob*: spit.
73 *bleeder*: stupid or contemptible person.
73 *burn*: cigarettes.
76 *grassed*: told the police.

Scene Eight
76 *choked off*: fed up.
79 *Always Charlie*: always me being a fool, as in the saying 'a right Charlie'.
80 *nancies*: slang for homosexuals.
85 *Put the wood in the 'ole*: close the door.

Scene Nine
90 *sinner-scope*: cinemascope (wide-screen films) had recently been introduced.
91 *shufties*: a look.
91 *'ave a bash*: have a go.

Scene Ten
95 *shag*: have sex.
96 *bangers*: sausages.

100   *clobbers 'im*: hits him.
100   *chokey*: normally means prison but here probably refers to solitary confinement.
100   *on yer jack*: on your own.
102   *pit*: bed.
102   *nosh*: food.
103   *tanner*: sixpence, the equivalent of 5p.
105   *land yer*: hit you.

Scene Eleven
110   *'Effin' and blindin'*: swearing continuously.

Scene Twelve
116   *ol' lag*: old habitual convict.
116   *ol' soak*: old drunkard/alcoholic.
119   *pop*: affectionate term for older man.

Terms Used by Bond

Accident Time: In an accident, the brain seems to slow down time, subjective time, to give us the possibility of dealing with the unexpected. The sense of slowness is caused by the brain concentrating with hypersensitivity. We notice more, often in uncanny detail, and see more objectively, because it can be a matter of life and death. It is as if we were in the stillness at the centre of a cyclone. In a play there can be extreme incidents, such as in *Saved* the infanticide and the last scene, when what is at stake is the meaning of what is happening, why it is happening. Then the usual routine accounts don't work and we ourselves must give the meaning. In the extreme this comes down to the meaning of the self: the meaning I give to the event is also the meaning I give to myself, because I am the sort of person who judges the event in this way. So, paradoxically, the incident shows me who I am. Accident Time cannot be created directly by artificially slowing down the action. The action may be made more specific or detailed or even speeded up. The audience, not the actors, go into Accident Time. The actors enable Accident Time to happen by understanding the play and using the various means and devices to enact their understanding.

Cathexing/decathexing: Bond borrows the term from Freud. In Freud it refers to the psychological energy something has when it becomes emotionally charged. Probably all objects are cathexed – for instance, even dust is cathexed with our mortality, so an ordinary dustpan could be used in a way that makes it as powerful as the skull Hamlet picks up. There is a critical use of cathexis in *Saved*: the baby is stoned to death. In biblical times stoning was a form of legal execution, the stone is the weapon of the righteous mob. Bond cathexes and decathexes objects to deprive them of their usual emotional hold over us and confront possible new meanings. It is like switching round texts under illustrations in a book. Or like turning a knife into a fork: it changes the action by changing its meaning. It's like switching round the functions of a set of chess pieces: the game becomes different. It's a matter not of imagery but of use, so that the audience are prompted into creativity. Cathexis can enhance or degrade an object and its use.

Drama Event/Theatre Event: The event in the play is made a Drama Event when the full significance of the moment is opened up. It is the analysis of the story. It is a moment of full emotional and intellectual involvement with the action by the audience which stimulates the imagination to seek reason. It is the opposite of Brecht's *Verfremdungseffekt* or 'alienation'.

Extreme: Bond takes the audience to extreme moments of human tension and conflict. This need not be physical or violent. It is a moment when the ordinary explanations break down. In *Saved* mending the chair is as extreme as breaking it. The extreme is often the occasion of Accident Time (q.v.).

The Gap: The gap is the space that opens up for us where we can create or deny human value. The aim of Bond's theatre is to place us in this gap, the site of our potential humanness, where the structure of the play and its enactment work in such a way that the ideological explanations society has given us are stripped away and we have to fill it with our own meaning. In that moment we can confirm or deny our humanness. In the stoning scene, if it has been enacted as the script demands, then the audience are placed in a relationship to the event where they can understand more of the society we are all creating or just condemn the young men. By its interpretation of the play's meaning and the use of various devices, the performance creates a gap the audience must enter. This is because the mind – like nature – abhors a vacuum.

Imagination: This is not the imaginary or fantasy. It is a fundamental function of the human mind. We have to interrogate events. We have to make meanings. It is a way of gaining knowledge. It sets up a search for reasons. We create ourselves in this way. In Bond's plays he is continually seeking to challenge our customary perceptions. He provokes and confronts us. In *Saved* does Harry see or not see Pam and Len in the first scene? Does he care or not care? Does he really exist?

Acting the Invisible Object: This is fundamental to Bond's drama and, perhaps, the most important device. Only the actor can create the IO, it depends on his or her understanding, sensitivity and awareness of the situation and on the artistic skill to re-create it.

The IO comes from the total involvement in a situation or moment and its meaning as it is disinterred from the whole play. It may use gesture, posture, expression, voice, movement, almost anything, and may show humanness or inhuman wickedness. It does not show the character's motive but the human motive, the motive to be human – so it is our common humanness made visible in human communication. When it is shown we must recognise it because it comes from our own Radical Innocence (q.v.). It may involve something as prominent as Len mending the chair or something as seemingly insignificant as putting down a cup or opening a door. Bond regards it as the actor's highest art.

Nothingness: Nothingness is the opposite of everything, and everything is full of 'somethings' – but nothingness is 'total'. It has no details. This makes it awesome. It's behind the comically nagging questions, 'What was there before there was anything?' and 'Why is there something rather than nothing?' From the beginning young children ask all the existential questions that probe nothingness. So nothingness seeps into everything. It is ideology's oldest colony, and guns and nothingness are its ultimate weapons. One way or another ideology makes nothingness the origin of creation and the secret meaning of everything, including ourselves. Authority claims that only it can know the meaning of something so important. But without a god to fill nothingness we have to find answers for ourselves. So it is the site of our imagination and humanness. Lear says 'Nothing will come of nothing', but everything comes from it. If we accept ideology's interpretation of it and the values it derives from it, then nothingness owns us.

Objects: Bond regularly uses common, everyday, mass-produced objects. Mostly they are already cathexed (q.v.) with values – for example in *Saved*, Mary's crockery. But he often cathects these objects with other values, sometimes using insignificant things to bear the highest values (the paradox of the stones in *Saved*). Another example is the discarded cigarette packet in *Great Peace*; the soldier seems to cathect it with his whole life and is shot for refusing to pick it up.

Radical Innocence: This is a completely different reading of the first stage of an infant's life from other interpretations. It is the fundamental building block of Bond's approach to drama. This RI is formed during the period when the baby is born and before it enters the cultural/social/historical world that it will encounter as language is first understood and then used. It encodes a basic striving to be at home in the world which forms the baby's imperative drive in later life. From this develops a basic sense of justice which is always there to be awakened. All Bond's devices focus on this aim. If justice is denied then humans must seek revenge.

A rather simplistic outline of Bond's new approach to form for the theatre of today could be seen as follows:

- The Drama/Theatre Event: moments in the play when the story is deconstructed to expose the social forces at work in that event. This means the play, the characters in the play and the audience have to be each on its own Site.
- Site or situation: where all the dimensions the play is exploring are made available. When we, the audience, enter the Site, through the DE (Drama Event), we are obliged to face/confront or ignore/confirm the ideology that we have become. The audience enters the Gap.
- The Gap: the area of no-man's land where our ideological props are taken away and we have to find ourselves. One of the means for this confrontation is the Invisible Object. Many of the devices may be used to create this confrontation.
- Invisible Object: the creative responsibility of the actor, to find how an action, object, gesture, in fact anything, can open the play's centre and evoke the DE. Objects are cathexed and decathexed.
- Cathexis: the device by which the emotional affects and meanings of objects and situations may be deconstructed or substituted by other affects and meaning.
- Accident Time: as in, for example, a car accident where the brain seems (by becoming more receptive) to slow everything down so that the mind seems to have more time to react and assess the situation, or (in drama) the meaning of the situation. At the same time this also defines the self because the self becomes the sort of self that makes this sort of judgement. The point of Accident Time is that it cancels out existing habitual ways of judging so that a new self may be chosen, be created. In Accident Time all the above work to reach the Radical Innocence of the audience.

- Radical Innocence: the area of the new infant's mind which forms what later becomes, in the real world, its human need for justice. When the infant consciously enters our world, the world of its minders, it encounters injustices and necessary expediencies. Then its need for justice may be compromised and even corrupted by its need to survive. But Radical Innocence remains potential in everyone because as infants we make it synonymous with being human. It is also the origin of human creativity, as opposed to the ability to contrive and 'manufacture'. Drama acts by confronting Radical Innocence in the adult, however residual it may have become. This is not a return to childhood, because when it is united with later experience RI becomes even more potent and definitive.
- Justice: the central pursuit of all serious drama.
- Enacting: 'Stop acting' is the often-heard comment of Bond to actors. Instead, Bond uses the term 'enacting'. This means not acting the character in the play but enacting the situation, the event, through which the social forces feeding that situation can be revealed. The drama devices are not meant to replace insight and intuition. They do not have to be used separately or in isolation but may be interrelated with each other. Together they produce this new way of acting which Bond calls enactment – this combines the stage 'Site' with the audience's Site, and by doing so turns the stage fiction into the audience's reality.

Questions for Further Study

1 Is the violence in the play gratuitous?
2 Does Bond have an 'ideology'?
3 Is Bond's authorial voice present in the play?
4 What role does the law play in *Saved*?
5 Who is most responsible for the murder of the baby?
6 Analyse the development of Scene Six step by step or, preferably, play it out with a group of people.
7 Is Len trying to be at home in the world or in society?
8 Is Bond justified in calling *Saved* 'almost irresponsibly optimistic'?
9 How many types of violence can be found in *Saved*?
10 What is the centre of *Saved* and what is the central line?
11 Write a letter responding to hate mail or harsh criticism about the play.
12 How many examples of everyday sayings are there in the play, by which people understand their lives? ('This is the life' is an example.) How many can you find around you in a twenty-four-hour period?
13 List all the examples of Len's positive actions in the play.
14 'Right-wing political violence cannot be justified because it always serves irrationality; but left-wing political violence is justified when it helps to create a more rational society, and when that help cannot be given in a pacific form' (Bond, Introduction to *Saved* in *Plays 1*). Discuss.
15 'Clearly the stoning to death of a baby in a London park is a typical English understatement. Compared to the "strategic" bombing of cities it is a negligible atrocity. Compared to the cultural and emotional deprivation of most children its consequences are insignificant' (Bond in Author's Note). Discuss.
16 Bond says that theatre cannot teach. Do you agree?
17 'The play is about a liberal and his failure to pacify his environment, in spite of his decency, tenderness and humanity' (Bond, letter to the *Guardian*, 12 November 1965) Discuss.
18 Why does Fred join in the stoning?

19   Why might Bond have described Len, in the list of characters, as having 'prominent feet'?

20   'I was [...] criticised for making the child-stoning in *Saved* "realistic" by people who firmly supported using the threat of nuclear weapons: gambling Russian roulette with not bullets but hydrogen rockets' (Bond). Discuss.

21   If the judge described Scene Six he would say: 'An event in which a baby was killed and a young man's jacket soiled.' If Mike described the scene he would say: 'An event in which my jacket was soiled and a baby killed.' What would this say about the judge, Mike and the city outside the park?

DAVID DAVIS is Professor of Drama in Education at Birmingham City University (formerly University of Central England) where he was the founder of, and until recently, director of the International Centre for Studies in Drama in Education and course leader for MA, MPhil and PhD studies in Drama in Education. At the university he now works only with his MPhil and PhD students and researches into Drama and Theatre in Education. He is also course director of a summer school in Jordan and teaches on the MA Drama in Education course at Trinity College, Dublin, where he is a research fellow. He taught for fifteen years as a drama teacher in secondary schools.

Methuen Drama Student Editions

Jean Anouilh *Antigone* • John Arden *Serjeant Musgrave's Dance*
Alan Ayckbourn *Confusions* • Aphra Behn *The Rover* • Edward Bond
Lear • *Saved* • Bertolt Brecht *The Caucasian Chalk Circle* • *Fear and
Misery in the Third Reich* • *The Good Person of Szechwan* • *Life of Galileo* •
Mother Courage and her Children • *The Resistible Rise of Arturo Ui* • *The
Threepenny Opera* • Anton Chekhov *The Cherry Orchard* • *The Seagull* •
Three Sisters • *Uncle Vanya* • Caryl Churchill *Serious Money* • *Top Girls*
• Shelagh Delaney *A Taste of Honey* • Euripides Elektra • *Medea* •
Dario Fo *Accidental Death of an Anarchist* • Michael Frayn *Copenhagen*
• John Galsworthy *Strife* • Nikolai Gogol *The Government Inspector* •
Robert Holman *Across Oka* • Henrik Ibsen *A Doll's House* • *Ghosts* •
Hedda Gabler • Charlotte Keatley *My Mother Said I Never Should* •
Bernard Kops *Dreams of Anne Frank* • Federico García Lorca *Blood
Wedding* • *Doña Rosita the Spinster* (bilingual edition) • *The House of
Bernarda Alba* • (bilingual edition) • *Yerma* (bilingual edition) • David
Mamet *Glengarry Glen Ross* • *Oleanna* • Patrick Marber *Closer* • John
Marston *The Malcontent* • Martin McDonagh *The Lieutenant of Inishmore* •
Joe Orton *Loot* • Luigi Pirandello *Six Characters in Search of an Author*
• Mark Ravenhill *Shopping and F***ing* • Willy Russell *Blood Brothers*
• *Educating Rita* • Sophocles *Antigone* • *Oedipus the King* • Wole
Soyinka *Death and the King's Horseman* • Shelagh Stephenson *The
Memory of Water* • August Strindberg *Miss Julie* • J. M. Synge *The
Playboy of the Western World* • Theatre Workshop *Oh What a Lovely
War* Timberlake Wertenbaker *Our Country's Good* • Arnold Wesker
The Merchant • Oscar Wilde *The Importance of Being Earnest* •
Tennessee Williams *A Streetcar Named Desire* • *The Glass Menagerie*

Methuen Drama Contemporary Dramatists

include

John Arden (two volumes)
Arden & D'Arcy
Peter Barnes (three volumes)
Sebastian Barry
Dermot Bolger
Edward Bond (eight volumes)
Howard Brenton
  (two volumes)
Richard Cameron
Jim Cartwright
Caryl Churchill (two volumes)
Sarah Daniels (two volumes)
Nick Darke
David Edgar (three volumes)
David Eldridge
Ben Elton
Dario Fo (two volumes)
Michael Frayn (three volumes)
David Greig
John Godber (four volumes)
Paul Godfrey
John Guare
Lee Hall (two volumes)
Peter Handke
Jonathan Harvey
  (two volumes)
Declan Hughes
Terry Johnson (three volumes)
Sarah Kane
Barrie Keeffe
Bernard-Marie Koltès
  (two volumes)
Franz Xaver Kroetz
David Lan
Bryony Lavery
Deborah Levy
Doug Lucie

David Mamet (four volumes)
Martin McDonagh
Duncan McLean
Anthony Minghella
  (two volumes)
Tom Murphy (six volumes)
Phyllis Nagy
Anthony Neilsen (two volumes)
Philip Osment
Gary Owen
Louise Page
Stewart Parker (two volumes)
Joe Penhall (two volumes)
Stephen Poliakoff
  (three volumes)
David Rabe (two volumes)
Mark Ravenhill (two volumes)
Christina Reid
Philip Ridley
Willy Russell
Eric-Emmanuel Schmitt
Ntozake Shange
Sam Shepard (two volumes)
Wole Soyinka (two volumes)
Simon Stephens (two volumes)
Shelagh Stephenson
David Storey (three volumes)
Sue Townsend
Judy Upton
Michel Vinaver
  (two volumes)
Arnold Wesker (two volumes)
Michael Wilcox
Roy Williams (three volumes)
Snoo Wilson (two volumes)
David Wood (two volumes)
Victoria Wood